MW00653092

FREEDOM STORIES

Untold Stories of
Round Rock, Texas

Published in Beaverton, Oregon, by Good Catch Publishing.
www.goodcatchpublishing.com
V1.1

Printed in the United States of America

Table of Contents

DEDICATION

This book is dedicated to those who have experienced circumstances in life that have left them feeling hopeless, addicted or trapped. If you need FREEDOM and desire to overcome and live a life that is worth living, then this book is for you!

ACKNOWLEDGEMENTS

I would like to thank Benito Fresquez for his vision for this book and his hard work in making it a reality. And to the people of Freedom, thank you for your boldness and vulnerability in sharing your personal stories.

This book would not have been published without the amazing efforts of our project manager and editor, Hayley Pandolph. Her untiring resolve pushed this project forward and turned it into a stunning victory. Thank you for your great fortitude and diligence. Deep thanks to our incredible editor in chief, Michelle Cuthrell, and executive editor, Jen Genovesi, for all the amazing work they do. I would also like to thank our invaluable proofreader, Melody Davis, for the focus and energy she has put into perfecting our words.

Lastly, I want to extend our gratitude to the creative and very talented Jenny Randle, who designed the beautiful cover for *Freedom Stories: Untold Stories of Round Rock, Texas.*

Daren Lindley
President and CEO
Good Catch Publishing

The book you are about to read
is a compilation of authentic life stories.
The facts are true, and the events are real.
These storytellers have dealt with crisis, tragedy, abuse
and neglect and have shared their most private moments,
mess-ups and hang-ups in order for others to learn and
grow from them. In order to protect the identities of those
involved in their pasts, the names and details of some
storytellers have been withheld or changed.

INTRODUCTION

What do you do when life is careening out of control? When addiction has overtaken you or abuse chained you with fear? Is debt escapable? Will relationships ever be healthy again? Are we destined to live as a prisoner of poor choices or difficult circumstances? Or will we ever be free?

The eight stories you are about to read prove positively that people right here in Round Rock have found FREEDOM.

Whether they'd been beaten down by abuse, broken promises, shattered dreams or suffocating addictions, the resounding answer is, "Yes! Your life really can change. It is possible to be FREE and become a new person."

The potential to break free from gloom and enter into a bright future awaits.

Expect inspiration, hope and transformation! As you walk with real people from our very own city through the pages of this book, you will not only find riveting accounts of their hardships, you will learn the secrets that brought about their breakthroughs.

These people are no longer living in the chains of yesterday. They are living FREE with a sense of purpose TODAY. May these stories inspire you to do the same.

STREET MUSIC
The Story of Raymond
Written by Karen Koczwara

I just want to die.

What's the point in even living?

A chilly rain pelted my cheeks as I pulled myself off the bench. I'd soon be soaked from head to toe if I didn't find a warm, dry place. I rubbed the sleep from my eyes.

My stomach rumbled, and I realized I hadn't eaten since the previous morning.

I'll have to see if I can score a piece of pizza tonight at that place down the street. At least that will tide me over for another day.

I shivered and brushed the rain from my cheeks, wishing again to just disappear.

Life is meaningless. I spend my days hopping from one place to another, scrambling for food, playing my guitar for a few bucks. I'm totally lost and broken. A real mess.

I've gotta get another fix. Get my hands on some drugs so I can escape my dreaded reality.

Numbness is the next best thing to death.

కళ కళ కళ

I was born in Texas on the eve of my father's high school graduation. My mother, a teenager as well, did not graduate with her class. My father worked in the construction business, and we moved all over Southern Texas for his well-paying job. But when his boss committed suicide, my father's work came to a halt, and he struggled to find steady employment. We moved in with my grandparents in the tiny rural town of El Ranchito, near the Mexican border, and my father worked in my grandfather's tire shop. As a lower-class Hispanic family in a town with little opportunity, we struggled to make ends meet.

My mother gave birth to two little girls, three years apart, and we became a family of five. My cousin, 10 years my senior, lived nearby, and we often played football in the vacant lot next to my grandparents' house. My peers began to bully me, hurling hurtful words like "Egghead!" in Spanish. My little body had not quite grown into my large head, making me an easy target for ridicule. I pretended their words didn't sting. In the meantime, I retreated and kept to myself. My parents drank regularly and spent a great deal of time away from home. To pass the time, I began helping my grandfather at the tire shop after school. We became especially close, and my grandfather affectionately called me his "favorite" and "little helper." His words comforted me much more than the cruel words on the sandlot.

My grandfather spoiled me with gifts when he could. When I turned 11, he taught me how to drive a car. One day he asked if I'd rather have a go-kart or a guitar as a special gift. I loved music and longed for a guitar of my own, but a go-kart sounded like lots of fun, too. I chose the wheels and spent my days exploring the great outdoors. I often got lost or stopped by a friend's house, not coming home until dark. My father complained to my grandfather about my free-spirited adventures.

"Oh, leave him alone," my grandfather said in my defense, waving away my father's concern. "He'll be just fine."

On my 12th birthday, my parents gave me a shiny new bike. I was elated, imagining the fun I'd have cruising up and down the streets. But the gift preceded a painful announcement: They were getting a divorce. My mother was tired of living with my grandparents and wanted a house of her own, as well as financial stability. She planned to move to Pflugerville, just outside Austin, with another man.

"Who do you want to live with?" my parents asked me.

At 12, on the brink of adolescence, these were not the choices I expected to make. I wanted to explore the town on my new bike and grow into my head. But I was now faced with something much more painful than taunting words. Our little family was splitting in two. I chose to live with my father, as I did not want him to be alone. My mother took my two sisters, and just like that, they were gone.

My grandfather passed away that year, and I mourned him deeply. He was well-known and well-loved in our little community, and I knew he would be missed by many, including me. Life suddenly felt cruel and unfair, and the humble little world I'd known became even less comforting. I began to ponder eternity, wondering what it must feel like to slip from life into death. Was there only darkness beyond the grave, or was there something else?

My father took over my grandfather's tire shop, and I hung out there in the afternoons, tinkering with the tools and machines. In middle school, I had begun to notice pretty girls, and I often fantasized about innocently holding hands with a girl while walking in the rain. The Doobie Brothers, Beach Boys and other popular tracks played softly in the background at the tire shop, and the melodies soothed me. *Someday I'll have a girl of my own. And someday everything will make sense.*

I cherished my time with my father. We watched the *Late Show with David Letterman* in the evenings and laughed in unison at the comedian's jokes. I followed him around the tire shop, taking note of everything he did. One day, he offered me a puff of his marijuana joint.

"You're gonna smoke it someday, anyway," he said nonchalantly.

Is he right? Is this my destiny?

With my grandfather and mother now gone, my grandmother and I became close. She treated me well, but if I got in trouble, she whooped me and rattled off words of warning in both Spanish and English. She took me to a small Baptist church with her on Sundays, and I sat in the back pew, taking it all in. As a shy kid, I didn't speak up much, but I finally worked up the courage to stand before the crowd and read Bible verses in Spanish. Eventually, I made a few friends in the teen Sunday school there. I still wasn't sure what to make of the whole God thing. Was he somewhere in the sky, waiting to whoop me like my grandmother if I messed up? Or was he the loving guy the pastor talked about?

I kept up my grades in middle school, scoring all A's on my report card. Football and track meets kept me busy, and I enjoyed my media technology classes as well. My interests varied from music to athletics to computers to girls, and singing brought me just as much pleasure as running the mile. But another world opened up to me during this time, too. My father's uncle, an alcoholic, became a strong influence in my life after my grandfather's death. We hung out in his living room, watching boxing on TV as he popped one beer after another. When the weather warmed, we trekked out to his boat and spent the afternoon fishing at the lake. Marijuana and booze always seemed to appear wherever we went. As a kid from a lower-class Hispanic family, I didn't think much of it. *This is just the way we roll around these parts. Everyone drinks. It's no big deal.*

I began high school, staying on top of my grades my freshman year. I loved learning and liked asking questions. I joined the Upward Bound program and enjoyed special extracurricular activities and field trips. My excellent test scores soon put me in the top 20 in my class.

Girls began to take notice of me my freshman year. Though I was intrigued by the opposite sex and often joked around with girls, my shyness still kept me from getting too close. One day, a pretty girl asked me to a school dance, and I politely declined. I did not know how to dance, and the idea of making a fool of myself in front of my peers made me cringe. Later, however, I accompanied a friend to her Quinceañera (15th birthday celebration) and learned how to move my two feet on the dance floor. As it turned out, it wasn't so scary after all.

Wanting to broaden my interests, I joined the school theater program. I enjoyed participating in one-act plays. My father also enrolled me in kung-fu classes, and though the experience didn't last long, I enjoyed learning a new skill. For a kid from a humble background, my future looked pretty promising and full.

I spent a great deal of time with my grandparents and cousins, who lived nearby. One of my cousins ran the sound for the school theater, and we spent a lot of time together. He always seemed to have a six-pack of beer around, and he handed me a can here and there. I enjoyed sipping the cool drink but wasn't interested in getting drunk. I had much more important things to do.

My sophomore year, I played football and took up track, long-distance running and boxing. I grew into my once-awkward body, and defined muscles suddenly appeared. I was now officially an athlete, and my peers took notice. The days of being bullied in the sandlot were now far behind me as I gained newfound respect.

Still an avid music lover, I decided to try out for band. I hoped to play drums, but the teacher handed me a trumpet instead. Disappointed, I decided to join choir. Singing was my first love and seemed to come easily for me. Even as a young boy, I'd loved to hum tunes, and my mother had often reminded me of my ability. Choir would be fun, I thought.

Not long after joining choir, I met a guy about my age. With dark hair and haunting eyes, he reminded me of Kurt Cobain, the lead singer from the band Nirvana. I was an avid grunge and heavy metal music fan, and the resemblance between the boy and the popular singer struck me in a powerful way.

"Hey, what's your name?" I hissed one day during choir.

The boy glanced up, his wide eyes meeting mine. "Excuse me?" He didn't seem rude or aloof.

He seems smart, I concluded. *And well mannered. I should get to know this guy.*

The boy and I began talking, and I learned he was a very talented musician who liked to rap and play instruments, as well as sing. But I soon discovered that beneath his proper exterior lay a secret dark side. One day, the boy introduced me to Everclear, a powerful 180-proof form of alcohol. I had only tasted beer and had no idea what to expect as I put the clear liquid to my lips. It was stronger than I expected, and I shuddered a bit as it trickled down my throat.

"That stuff will get you drunk real fast," my new friend informed me with a knowing look. From that moment on, I dubbed him Mr. Everclear.

Mr. Everclear quickly led me into a strange, sinister world, one in which drugs, booze and women flowed freely. I began sleeping around, and my new friend and I shared women just as casually as we shared our drugs. Though I'd smoked pot a few times with my family, I now graduated to harder drugs, like cocaine. It seemed there was nothing Mr. Everclear could not get his hands on. We continued to play music together but spent most of our days high or drunk. I often blacked out, not remembering large chunks of time. My grades quickly slipped, and I no longer cared about school. Mr. Everclear's world was exciting and grown-up, and I didn't want to return to the land of innocence. I was a man now. Or so I thought.

I began partying regularly, getting wasted on the weekends and at school. I found a local liquor store that sold booze to minors and often hit it up before parties. My friends and I stole alcohol from our parents' liquor cabinets as well. I continued doing cocaine, even trading a night of cheap sex in exchange for the drug. Life in my small town now felt exciting, and I liked it.

When I turned 16, I left my father's new house and moved back in with my grandmother. I stayed in the bedroom at the back of her house, which had its own private entrance to the backyard. I snuck girls in and out, and my grandmother never caught on. Once, after drinking too much, I puked and urinated on myself in my bed. When my grandmother found me lying in the stench the next morning, she simply said, "Get up." I wasn't sure if she'd caught on to my troublesome ways or if she was completely naïve. Either way, I decided I'd have my fun as long as I could.

STREET MUSIC

I kept in touch with my mother, visiting her in the summer when my father went off hunting with his friends. She had moved to Austin, several hours away, and had two more daughters with her new man. I wasn't sure how I fit in her new life and wasn't sure I wanted to be a part of it, anyway. *I know she's onto me. She thinks I'm trouble, but I don't really care. No one can control me now. I'm almost a grown-up.*

Mr. Everclear became my primary role model. The more time I spent with the guy, the more I wanted to emulate him. I watched his every move, impressed by how he dressed, talked and acted. He possessed a charismatic charm, and our peers took notice of his fun, extroverted personality. It seemed he knew how to make everyone laugh. Some seniors on campus even wrote a humorous skit called "What Would Mr. Everclear Do?" I hung out in his shadow, grateful he'd chosen me as his faithful sidekick. As he cocked his head to the side and erupted in laughter, a crowd gathering around him, I reminded myself of his secret dark side. *This guy is trouble, but he's also popular, and I want to be like him. Maybe I'm even a little jealous. Either way, right now, I'm having fun.*

At school, I worked through modules at my own pace, keeping up with algebra and reading. But my grades continued to slip, and though I remained active with sports for a while, I eventually lost interest. The more drugs I did, the more withdrawn I became. I began drinking and snorting cocaine at school, getting my hands on the stuff every chance I got. I eventually transferred to

FREEDOM STORIES

another high school and joined the choir there. But my grades continued to suffer, hovering just above passing. Trouble followed me there. After I exposed myself to a girl and got caught with pot, the principal kicked me out and sent me off to an alternative school. I eventually lost contact with Mr. Everclear, the boy who'd tempted me down that dark path.

The administrators at the alternative school meant business. They shaved my long, dark hair off and tried to whip me into shape, reminding me I would not graduate if I did not adhere to their rules. I did the bare minimum to pass my classes and managed to graduate. My school counselors helped me apply to colleges, and I decided to head to San Antonio to further my education. But books weren't really on my mind. I just wanted to escape my small town and get to the big city, where the real fun could begin.

After just a semester of college in San Antonio, I pocketed the financial aid money and dropped out. I landed a job at a fast-food barbecue place and secured my own apartment. Now an independent man, I decided to do whatever I pleased. I began smoking and selling crack and soon learned most of the tenants in my apartment complex were druggies as well. The days became a blur, as people drifted in and out of my apartment, some looking for a quick deal, and others looking for a place to crash. The boy who once sang in the choir, sprinted on the track field and dreamed of innocently holding a girl's hand now faded far into the distance, replaced by someone I hardly recognized. Life now revolved around getting high and staying high. Numbness remained the ultimate goal.

"You ever shot up coke before?" one of my new friends asked.

I shook my head. "Nope."

"Oh, man, so much better than smoking it. You gotta try it," he insisted. He showed me how to shoot up, and my eyes bulged as he plunged the needle into his arm.

I tried shooting up coke and quickly realized he was right. The high hit almost instantly, proving different than anything I'd ever tried. Next, I learned how to cook crack. On the learning scale of drugs, I was quickly catching on. *Wow, the possibilities are endless,* I realized. *This is really crazy.*

One day, as I smoked crack with some friends in my apartment, a guy began shooting up heroin. "Hit me up, bro," I told him. *Why not?*

While shooting up crack had felt good, heroin felt even better. The drug was more powerful than anything I'd ever experienced. Within minutes, I felt numb, safe and warm, like a soft security blanket had been wrapped tightly around me. *Now this is the real deal. This, I could get used to.*

The next few months were a whirlwind of drugs, booze and partying. Strangers showed up at my apartment day and night, and I offered them what they needed or took what they had. One girl told me she'd give me her body in exchange for crack. I'd once been afraid to dance with a girl or even speak to the opposite sex, and I now found myself willing to trade cheap sex in exchange for a quick high. People of all ages and races floated in and out of my life. I didn't know most of their names, and I didn't take the time to memorize their faces. Most of the time, I was too high on crack or heroin to care about anything or anyone but myself.

I held various retail and restaurant jobs, working at places like Payless and IHOP. Even while high, I managed to perform my duties well. In my spare time, I ventured out to musical shows. Music still remained my solace, my escape, and I hoped to one day fit it in my life again. But drugs were taking over my existence, replacing my dreams as they sucked me further and further into darkness.

My mother came to visit once in a while, and I knew my living conditions disturbed her. My dirty little one-bedroom apartment had become a drug hot spot, and my friends were not the most reputable folks in town.

I did not own a car and relied on friends or bus transportation to get around town. I'd dropped out of college, squandering my smarts that could have landed me a promising career. The shy, curious boy of my youth was replaced by a hardened kid who liked heroin. I saw my mother's disappointed eyes as she looked me over, knowing what she must be thinking.

I've hurt you, Mom, I thought. *And I'm sorry. But I'm not ready to give this up right now. I'm just having a little fun.*

One night, my friend and I ventured out to score some heroin. My friend had a warrant out for his arrest, and he had been drinking before hopping behind the wheel of his car. When we heard sirens blaring behind us, I froze in my seat. *Cops. S***.*

"Dude, the drugs," my friend croaked, panic blazing in his eyes.

"I'll take care of it." I grabbed the $40 worth of heroin, shoved it in my mouth and swallowed it just as the cop approached the car window.

The cop arrested my friend and hauled him off to jail. I took the bus home that night, breathing a sigh of relief that the cop hadn't arrested me as well. From then on, I had a difficult time scoring heroin. I resorted to drinking booze and focused on my graveyard job at IHOP. I continued to sell crack and moved on to another part-time job. But my partying ways got in the way of my work duties. I eventually lost my job and could not pay the rent on my dingy apartment. I packed what few belongings I owned and moved out of the place, leaving behind a trail of vandalism. Holes in the walls remained, a reminder of many late-night drunken fights. Stained carpet and broken appliances told a story of a lack of care in my dark, drug-filled world. It was time to get out of there, but where would I go next?

One of my friends, also a heavy drug user, found us a tiny room to rent downtown, and we holed up there for a while. We continued doing drugs, and after moving out of that room, we crashed at rundown motels. We began shoplifting, stealing MP3 players, calculators and other electronics from Walmart and Target. My friend and I became adept at stealing, changing clothes often and disguising ourselves so the security cameras would not identify us. We ate peanut butter sandwiches to get by, and when our stomachs still rumbled, we trudged down to the local grocery store to steal some food. On several occasions, we dined and dashed, eating fancy meals at fine restaurants and then running for the door before the bill arrived. I enjoyed the thrill, but my heart still raced a bit every time we ran for the bus stop as the restaurant employees chased after us.

After shoplifting one day, a plainclothes cop caught and arrested me. He hauled me off to jail, and I spent the next week behind bars. After a court hearing, they released me back onto the streets. With nowhere to go, I returned to my grandmother's house, hoping she'd take me back in.

I had nothing but a suitcase and a guitar when I sheepishly showed up on my grandmother's front porch. She welcomed me back in with open arms. I knew my grandmother had always believed in me. She had dreamed for me when I could not dream, convinced I'd be married and prosperous someday. I wasn't so sure about that, though. I knew I was in trouble, but I still wasn't ready to change my ways. I lived for getting high, and drugs had become my best friend. Little else mattered.

Within no time, I met some new friends in her little town and began drinking and doing coke again. Drugs were never hard to find, no matter where I went. My cousin hooked me up with a job at Subway, where he worked as a manager. My friend from the city showed up on a bus not long after, looking for some coke. We got high and drunk together, resuming our old ways. Before long, we took up shoplifting again as well.

"I don't like that guy," my grandmother told me disapprovingly.

I was 19, and my friend was 10 years my senior. I understood her concern but wanted her to mind her own business, too. *I can live my own life, Grandma. I'm an adult now, and you can't tell me what to do.*

My friend settled in the town, and we became inseparable again. The more drugs we used, the more paranoid we became.

My friend got a gun, and when people came to the door of his place, he threatened to shoot them. I spent less and less time at my grandmother's, wanting my own independence. But after the cops showed up at my friend's door one day, I decided to go back to her house.

I didn't hear from my friend for a few weeks, and he finally called to say he was in Washington. "You should move up here, man. Get out of Texas for good. It's really cool up here," he said, persuading me.

What the heck? Maybe it would be good to get out of Texas, at least for a while. I don't have much going for me here, anyway. I picked up a few cartons of cigarettes across the Mexican border and hopped on a bus headed north. My friend and his sister picked me up at the bus station in the Tacoma area a few days later.

My friend and I bunked with his sister and spent our days drinking and smoking pot. Washington, though beautifully green and lush, was especially rainy and depressing, and our routine quickly got old. When his sister kicked us out, we drove drunk down to Portland, confused as to where to go next.

"What now?" I asked my friend, lighting up a cigarette.

"I guess we're outta here. We can head south. Do a road trip, and see where we end up," he replied with a shrug.

We made our way down to Redding, California, a couple hours south of the Oregon border. With no money for a hotel, we holed up at a Salvation Army shelter for the night. There, I met a woman several years older than me. She seemed pleasant enough, and when I asked her for a cigarette, she handed me the whole pack. The three of us pooled what little money we had and got a motel for the next two nights. We spent the evening drinking and discussing what to do next.

"Do you want to go to my mom's house? She lives down in the Sacramento area," the woman asked us.

It sounded like as good a plan as any to me. We headed to Sacramento, where we met the woman's mother and family. They offered to let us stay with them for the time being. I was grateful for their generosity and hospitality, as we had nowhere else to go. Desperate to get my hands on some booze again, I stole whiskey from the local grocery store. The woman stuck to her drug of choice — valium. We remained there for a month — an odd trio of dysfunctional strangers under one roof.

I soon learned the woman's family were Christians.

STREET MUSIC

They went to church every Sunday and invited us to come along. Having nothing better to do, I decided to check it out. The service was nice, the people were kind and the food afterward was a surprising treat. I hadn't set foot in a church since I'd gone with my grandmother as a child. I remembered standing up in the teen Sunday school class, reciting Bible passages in Spanish. God remained a mystery to me, but his people seemed pretty cool. Though I didn't have any long-terms plans to become a Christian myself, I wasn't opposed to hearing more about this God stuff someday. But right now, I figured, I just needed to focus on the basics and figure out a survival plan.

My two friends and I hung out together, listening to music and enjoying each other's company. My friend from the city eventually landed a job and decided to stay in the area. But I didn't see my future in California and decided to head back to Texas. The woman bought me a bus ticket, and I thanked her and said my goodbyes.

Having lived in some seedy areas throughout my life, I had been exposed to a great deal of crime, drugs and danger. But nothing could have prepared me for the Oakland Greyhound bus station. Bulletproof glass windows separated the ticket clerks from the passengers, and I waited for my bus for hours, watching a stream of rough-looking people saunter by. Inside, I felt like a scared little kid, but I tried to look cool, drowning out the hollering in my head as I waited for the bus to arrive. At last, the Greyhound rounded the corner, and I hopped on, relieved to get out of there. *Adventure's over. Time to go home. I don't know what's next, but there's nothing for me here.*

I returned to my grandmother's house and tried to resume normal life. "Hey, *mijo*," she said, greeting me warmly at the door, just as she had before. I welcomed her familiar embrace after a long, scary and uncomfortable bus ride. A night in a warm bed would hopefully do the trick and revive me again.

But sleep did not come easily. I tossed and turned, unable to drift off. Mood swings began to plague me, and I grew confused and anxious. *What's going on with me? I'm a wreck!*

My parents learned I was back in town, and they soon grew concerned with my behavior. "What's going on, Raymond?" they asked. "You don't seem well at all."

I began partying again, drinking and smoking large amounts of pot. I managed to stay away from heroin but grew paranoid nonetheless. My panic attacks worsened, and at last, I decided to see a doctor about my troubling condition.

"I think you are struggling with bipolar disorder," he informed me.

Bipolar? I'm only 20! Do I really have a mental illness? The idea frightened me, but instead of cleaning up my life, I turned to booze and drugs. Soon, I began snorting coke again. Coke and booze proved the perfect recipe for disaster. Nothing brought out my demons faster than a mixture of the two substances. Coupled with my already fragile mental state, I was in real trouble.

STREET MUSIC

High on coke and drunk on booze, I called my cousins' house one night and lashed out, threatening to hurt them. I then drove out to El Ranchito and showed up on their property. Afraid I'd come to harm them, my two cousins marched outside, whipped out their guns and promptly shot at me five times. I crumpled to the ground, writhing in pain. *What the h*** just happened?*

The family called for help, and a helicopter arrived a short time later. The paramedics airlifted me to the nearest hospital, where they treated my wounds. I'd been shot twice in the leg, once in my left knee, once in my hand and once in the stomach. I spent the next two weeks in the hospital, undergoing reconstructive surgery and trying to heal. When my father first saw me right after the shooting, he was relieved to find me alive.

"You could have been killed, Raymond," he said gravely, shaking his head. "I'm just glad you're all right."

I was grateful to see my father's face and grateful to be alive. But by now the physical pain had trickled straight to my heart, and I began to relive the prior few years in my mind. I thought of my grandfather, so kind, so well-loved by everyone he met. A gaping hole had formed in my heart when he died. He'd believed in me, and with him around, I felt safe, secure and understood. But after his death, everything had fallen apart.

My parents, overwhelmed by finances and differences of opinion, had parted ways, and I'd lost the comfort of having my mother around. Even a shiny bike and a go-kart did little to ease the heartache.

FREEDOM STORIES

I'd tried throwing myself into my studies, using music, sports and girls to distract me from my pain. For a while, life seemed like it might veer back on track. But Mr. Everclear had sucked me into his dark world, and I was too intrigued to escape. I'd then spent a few years flailing, hopping from job to job and town to town, always looking for a quick high. Life felt meaningless and empty, but I didn't know how to change. Getting shot should have been a wake-up call to get things together, but instead, I simply returned to my partying ways the moment the doctors released me from the hospital.

I turned 21, and a whole new world opened up to me. I was suddenly legal and could saunter into any bar I wanted. Booze and drugs abounded. My mother, eager to see me drastically change, suggested I move to Austin. The bustling city offered an eclectic range of musical opportunities, and I still loved to play the guitar. She hoped a change of scenery might help me turn my life right-side up.

I moved to Austin, found a job and moved into a hotel. Three months later, I secured an apartment of my own. Within no time, I met coke addicts, and we began hanging out. I often wandered over to a park in downtown Austin and bought drugs from several homeless guys. We smoked and snorted crack, and I took up heroin again. I had developed a love/hate relationship with heroin, convinced I could not live with or without it. The drug had cast a spell over me, and under its power, I felt helpless.

STREET MUSIC

One evening, after drinking and snorting coke, I overdosed. My lips turned completely purple, and my face abruptly smacked the ground. My friends called the paramedics, and an ambulance arrived and whisked me off to the emergency room. I awoke later in the hospital to find several tubes shoved down my throat. It was a terrible, suffocating feeling. When I glanced up, I saw my mother looking down at me. She did not cry, but the hollow look in her eyes said it all. *When is enough enough, Raymond? What are you doing to yourself?*

The doctors explained I'd overloaded my system and warned me to take better care of myself. I knew I was lucky — I had now encountered death's door twice. I was playing Russian roulette, and next time, things might not work out in my favor. But I didn't really care. Drugs had a hold over me, and I wasn't ready to give them up yet.

I lost my job and soon got evicted from my apartment. I now faced homelessness. *I am in the real world now,* I realized, fear seizing me. *No one is going to come running to save me. I've got to figure this out. I'll find a way to get by.*

I began panhandling for money on the streets, sleeping in vacant houses, under bridges, in fields or wherever I could safely curl up for the night. Many times, I awoke shivering as the chilly rain pelted my cheeks. I met several street gang members and remained thankful that they left me alone. When food ran scarce, I showed up at a local pizza place, where the owner dished out free slices of pizza at night. Sometimes, I played my guitar and sang on sidewalks to make a few bucks. On an especially good night, I counted $100 after my performance. I had gone from a talented, bright kid in a small town to a lonely, lost homeless guy on the streets of Austin. And nobody seemed to care.

Depression set in, as the reality of my situation hit me with full force. *I am alone. No one knows my name. I am a washed-up junkie who sleeps in the rain and relies on free slices of pizza to keep from going hungry. I am hopeless and tired of living. I would be better off dead.*

When winter set in, I checked into rehab, but I only lasted a couple days. Hallucinations plagued me as I tried to sober up, and I soon returned to the streets. My days became an endless cycle of attempting to survive, as I hopped from place to place in search of a warm place to sleep and a few crumbs to settle my growling stomach. I hated my life, hated who I had become. I thought about the tire shop and the Doobie Brothers and holding hands with a girl in the rain. It all seemed like a pipe dream now, completely unattainable. In my mid-20s, I felt like my life had come to an end. Digging my way out of the mess this time would be too difficult.

I began to ask the bigger questions. *Why, God?* As I lay under the stars and stared up at the vast sky above, I wondered if God really existed. And if he did exist, did he really care about a messed-up guy like me?

Despite my circumstances, I still attempted to maintain relationships with my family. My sister lived nearby, and I visited her once in a while and used the

Internet in her apartment clubhouse. One day, as I browsed the computer, a man wandered into the room. He struck up a conversation with me, and I responded to his questions politely. *This guy seems nice enough,* I thought.

I ran into the guy several more times. He introduced himself as Benito and finally told me he was a pastor of a local church. *A pastor! Wow! If only he knew I'm a drug user and a drunk. What would he think then?*

"We'd love to have you visit our church sometime," Benito said with a smile. "It's called Freedom Church, and we meet in Round Rock."

Church. Hmm. I mulled over the idea for a moment, remembering the nice church folks back in California. *It wasn't that scary. In fact, it was kind of nice, like having another family to belong to. I wouldn't mind checking out Benito's church. After all, he seems like a cool guy. And what do I have to lose, anyhow? I'm a junkie on the streets, with no job and no true friends. This could be okay.*

I continued struggling mentally with my moods and thought processes. The doctors handed me a new diagnosis: schizoaffective disorder.

The disorder, characterized by both schizophrenic and bipolar symptoms, seemed to define my struggles to a tee. Substance abuse was a likely reason why I'd become susceptible. I began receiving disability checks for my disorder and was able to secure housing. At last, I no longer faced chilly nights on the streets.

Though disturbed by the diagnosis, I kept using drugs. I continued visiting my sister's apartment complex and running into Benito. He gently invited me to church, and at last, I told him I'd go.

I showed up at Freedom Church, not sure what to expect as I walked through the doors. To my relief, everyone was especially friendly. I listened as Pastor Benito preached, appreciating the way he made the Bible verses clear and understandable. *He speaks as though we're sitting together having coffee. I like this. I want to find out more about the Bible and really dig in, see what this stuff is all about.*

I began lingering after church, getting to know a few of the members over lunch. They embraced me as though I'd been attending a long time. *These people are cool. They're real people with real struggles, just like me. They're so kind, and they don't seem to judge me. Maybe I could do this church thing after all.*

I attended Freedom Church, enjoying it more and more each week. Pastor Benito spoke about a God of love, a God of second chances. His words resonated with me. I thought about the many messed-up things I'd done over the years. Benito explained that Jesus had paid the price for the wrong things we'd done when he died on the cross. Because of his sacrifice, we could spend eternity with him in heaven if we surrendered our lives to him. We did not have to live in bondage to our problems, but instead, just as the church's name suggested, we could be free. *This is really good news,* I realized. *I can't do this on my own, but with God's help, I could be free of this lifestyle I've been tangled up in for so long.*

Instead of focusing on socializing, I holed up in my room, poring over the Bible and learning as much as I could. I was fascinated by the stories of Jesus that Pastor Benito talked about. When I could not sleep, I flipped on the light and cracked open my Bible, eager to dive in. Tears poured down my cheeks. I read about a thief who hung next to Jesus on a cross. The thief turned to Jesus and said, "Remember me." And Jesus told him he'd see him in heaven. *Wow, just like that, Jesus forgave him. The thief didn't have time to do anything good with his life, but he cried out to Jesus, and Jesus rescued him. He gave him hope. I want that hope. I know I am lost, flailing and completely broken. Could Jesus rescue a guy like me?*

The more I read the Bible, the more I became convinced it was the truth. Suddenly, it all made sense to me. *Jesus is the answer. This is the real deal. Jesus, I accept you into my heart. I now know you are the missing piece, the one I've been searching for my whole life. I know you are the only one who can pull me out of this ugly pit. I need your help. Please intervene in my life and rescue me. Forgive me for the wrong I've done. I want to live for you from now on.*

And Jesus did. I wouldn't have believed it possible, but he rescued me and filled me with his strength, and I sobered up. I continued attending Freedom Church and enjoyed the newfound freedom I'd found in Jesus. *I've beat this drug-ridden lifestyle that's trapped me for so long. I don't need that stuff anymore! I have something better. I have a relationship with Jesus now. I have that hope I've been searching for. I am not alone.* It was the best feeling in the world, like pulling off heavy shackles that had kept me in bondage all my life. *I am a new person now!*

Pastor Benito continued to encourage me, showering me with love. He treated me as a friend, even inviting me over for Thanksgiving dinner. I thought of the many so-called friends I'd met on the streets, friends who had used me just to get their next fix. *Those weren't true friends. They didn't really care about me, my future or my heart. But Pastor Benito does — I can tell. He really wants to see me thrive. And I appreciate that.*

In April 2012, I attended a friend's wedding. I saw a neighbor friend there, and we began drinking together. From there, I relapsed and began using heroin again. Heroin had always been my first love, like a girlfriend I knew was bad news but could not stay away from. The moment I plunged the needle into my arm, the familiar numbness and happiness set in again. *Ahh. This feels good.*

Meth sucked me in again as well. Before long, I was drinking and using both meth and heroin. My friend from high school came to visit, and we spent our days getting high. My weight plummeted to an astonishing 130 pounds, and I transformed into a walking skeleton. I tried to get help, but each time I did, I relapsed. By wintertime, I was psychotic. I called the cops one night, screaming into the phone. They dragged me to the hospital, but the minute I got out, I relapsed yet again. I moved to another apartment and tried another program, but it failed to help. In just a short amount of time, my life again had gone completely out of control.

I called Pastor Benito, completely broken. "I relapsed, man," I told him through tears. "I'm totally messed up again."

But Pastor Benito did not give up on me. Instead, he reassured me, telling me he was praying for me and that it was not too late to turn my life around. "You have Jesus, and he is your strength now, Raymond. You can beat this. You are strong."

I hated the fact that I'd relapsed, but I wasn't sure how to get away from drugs once and for all. They beckoned to me, luring me with temporary feelings of numbness and pleasure. Could a street junkie like me ever get completely clean? Was there any hope for me?

At last, I found a decent rehab program. The place proved much different than the rest, and when I walked out those doors, I knew something had changed. I was sober and had no intention of going back to my dark ways. With God's help, I was a new man.

I returned to Freedom Church and began getting more involved. Pastor Benito remained by my side as my biggest cheerleader, encouraging me not to focus on my past. "Tomorrow is a new day," he reminded me. "And God's mercy is new every day."

The more I read my Bible, the more I understood

grace. I had heard the word used over the years, but now, as a new believer in Jesus Christ, I finally understood the implications. Grace meant that God had lavished his love on me, even when I did not deserve it. His grace, as Benito said, sometimes seemed too good to be true. How could an amazing God, the creator of the universe, pick up guys like me and love them unconditionally? The idea was almost scandalous, it was so hard to fathom.

But as I pored over the passages in the Bible, I learned about several other guys like me. A man named David had messed up pretty badly, even having his mistress' husband killed. Another man named Paul had once hated Christians and had them put to death. But both of those men had discovered the same grace I had, and as they asked for forgiveness, Jesus wiped their slate clean. God even referred to David, once a murderer, as a man after his own heart. *Wow, God! Your grace really does stretch far and wide. You really are the God of second chances. Thank you for giving me one.*

Today, I am sober and happy. I eat right, exercise and take my medication. I love spending time at Freedom Church and hope to get even more involved, perhaps playing on the worship team someday. I have not forgotten the boy who hummed along to the Doobie Brothers in my grandfather's tire shop, the kid who sang in the school choir and the young man who strummed his guitar on the streets of Austin. I know God has given me the gift of music, and I would like to use it for him. Perhaps God will even bless me with a wife to share my life with someday, and if I'm lucky, she might like to make music, too.

Sometimes, as I glance over the stunning Austin skyline, taking in the bright city lights, I think about the guy I was not very long ago. As a lonely kid from a little farm town, I turned to drugs and alcohol to numb my pain. I spent a good chunk of my life lost and broken, looking to the things of the world to fill the gaping hole in my heart. At times, I wanted to pull myself out of the darkness, but I simply didn't know how. Only Jesus was able to rescue me. Through his power and love, I finally rose out of that ugly pit and made a permanent change. I know I will still struggle with temptation, but thanks to Pastor Benito and my wonderful new friends at Freedom Church, I know I will not face my battles alone. I have a new family now. I am no longer a druggie on the streets. I have found a place to call home.

WHY ME?
The Story of Ken
Written by Angela Welch Prusia

Tick, tick, tick.

Time taunted me.

Every second drove me to work like a madman. I pressed my limits in a rush against the clock.

The heat index pushed the temperature to 111 degrees. Sunrays bathed the concrete around me, hardening the wet grey mix into white stone.

Sweat beaded my face and dripped down my back. Thirst burned my throat, but I didn't break for water. A muscle cramp made me stumble.

You can do it, I told myself. *Just a little bit longer.*

I'd been a fool to attempt to complete this job without help from the guys. But I was too stubborn to reschedule the work order when one after another employee called in sick.

Fuzzy lines blurred my vision. My heart fired in rapid succession. I ignored the signs of heat exhaustion and pressed to the point of no return.

Why had I let the concrete truck leave? I was completely alone.

I yelled for help, but the words wouldn't launch past my brain. Concrete gripped my ankles in a vice. My brain screamed for my feet to move.

But my weakened state was no match for the physical properties of setting concrete.

Panic rose like bile, strangling me with fear.

I toppled over at a strange angle. My head dipped. Wet concrete filled an ear, one nostril and half my mouth. The only thing I could do was hit speed dial on my cell phone.

"Hey, babe." My wife's voice came over the line.

When I didn't answer, concern took over. "Ken? Are you there?"

Help me! I shrieked in silence.

"Ken, where are you? Stay on the line. I'm calling 911."

It would do no good. She'd never find me in time. I was drowning in concrete.

After Samuel's accident, I'd begged God to take my life.

But now, staring death in the face, I wanted to live. My new wife and I had dreams for our life together. *Please, God, don't let me die.*

Scenes from my life flashed before my eyes.

స్త్రస్త్రస్త్ర

"Ready to come home?" The woman with salt-and-pepper hair knelt beside me.

I studied the unfamiliar face, wary of another stranger. Trauma in my first three years of life left me guarded. A German shepherd ripped my eye out of the socket before my first birthday. Miraculously the doctor saved my eye. There was no explanation for my perfect vision. Not long after, my mother's new husband beat me so badly I spent days in the ICU until the swelling on my brain lessened. I should have died.

My foster mom nudged me forward. "Go on. Give your grandmother a hug."

I took a tentative step forward, and the woman wrapped a leathery hand around mine. Spidery blue veins lined her skin.

A baby cried from inside the house. "I have to go." My foster mom waved to me. "Goodbye, Ken."

The door shut, severing yet another tie. I had no choice but to follow the new woman.

Fifteen minutes later, I climbed the steep steps onto a bus. The driver gave me a toothy grin. Grandma chose a seat near the front and patted the spot next to her.

I hopped next to her, my legs dangling off the edge. I scooted forward, but I couldn't reach the rubber floor mat. I strained my neck to see out of the window. Skyscrapers soon turned to a long stretch of desert.

"Do you like animal crackers?" Grandma handed me a large bag of cookies.

My eyes widened in surprise. "For me?" Nothing belonged to me that wasn't shared by other foster kids.

She opened the package and set it on my lap. "All yours."

I couldn't believe my luck. Sweets were a luxury I had yet to experience. I marched a lion into my mouth, delighted with the taste.

The bag lasted the entire trip. Soon Grandma pointed

to a green population sign on the edge of the city. "Look. We're in El Paso."

The freeway dipped under another highway. My gaze followed the twists of the cloverleaf exits, wondering which road led to my new home.

҈҈҈

The mulberry trees outside Grandma's house made my heart leap as I approached her house for the first time. I imagined myself lost in the leafy branches for hours.

"Hey, nephew." A girl who looked to be about high school age welcomed me. "Want to see my Hot Wheels collection?"

She led me into her room where racks of display cases captivated me. I stared at a shiny sports car enclosed by plastic.

"You like the Chevelle?"

I wanted to hold the car in my hand and trace my fingers along the metal.

"I have a feeling we're going to be great friends." She nudged me. "I'm Genevieve."

A strange warm feeling swelled inside me. I'd never bonded so quickly with anyone.

"Want to see your room?" Genevieve started down the hall, and I padded down the carpet behind her. A single metal Army bed was pushed against the wall. *Did I really have a room to myself?*

Life would've been perfect had it not been for the

WHY ME?

angry giant married to my grandmother. My grandfather, a night security guard, intimidated me from the moment I met him. At 6 feet, 7 inches and 300 pounds, he towered over me.

The first time he took me to collect aluminum cans, we stopped off at a secluded back road, and he robbed me of my innocence. Terrified and ashamed, I kept the secret locked inside.

The sound of his footsteps made me shrink in fear. When my grandfather didn't force me out of the house to collect cans, he beat me whenever my grandmother wasn't around to protect me. He'd swing his steel-toed work boots over my body until the metal met skin. Pain coursed through my body like fire. Blood smeared the back of my head and shoulders.

Fighting back was futile. My grandfather would sit on top of me and pelt my back until my body went limp. The aftermath left me bruised for days. When I started school, my teachers would scold me for hunching over in my seat. Leaning back against the seat inflamed the pain.

Not long before I started kindergarten, my mom moved into my grandmother's home, her belly swollen with my half-brother. A crib and bunk bed now crowded my bedroom. Her failed relationship with the man who landed me in the ICU consumed her. She couldn't have cared less about me.

૨૦૨૦૨૦

FREEDOM STORIES

I loved going to church with my grandmother. No one ever took the time to read or sing to me at home. Stories from the Bible captivated me as my teacher illustrated the action with characters on a felt storyboard.

"Stop and let me tell you what the Lord has done," I sang, while holding a stop sign in my hand. The rocket song was my favorite. I blasted off into the air for Jesus.

When my teacher told us God's son died to forgive our sins so we could live forever in heaven, I wanted to become a Christian. I could identify with Jesus because of the suffering he endured. The next week, I sat in "big church" with the adults.

"These boys and girls have made an important decision," the pastor told the crowd, and everyone clapped.

My heart swelled when I got my very own Bible.

❧❧❧

"Why are you playing with matches, boy?" My grandfather cornered me in the living room after school one day. I cowered in front of him, bracing myself for the blows.

"I'm sorry," I pleaded.

"Sorry?" He grabbed his boots and started swinging. "You're a sorry excuse for life."

Metal cracked against bone. Pain shot through my skull. I crumpled to the floor, clutching the side of my head.

WHY ME?

"What are you doing?" My mom had come home early and soon broke into hysterics. She hadn't witnessed his abuse of me before, and terror had kept me silent. Their yelling match made my head throb.

"Pack your things, Ken. We're not staying here another day."

"I'm coming with you." Genevieve walked into the room and allied herself with us. Defiance lit her eyes with determination. We never talked about the abuse we both endured.

Surprise trumped my pain. I had to pinch myself. *Was escape finally possible?*

కింకింకిం

Mom's minimum wage jobs barely paid the bills, but I didn't complain. Sleeping on the floor in a sleeping bag was better than living with my grandfather's rage.

Unfortunately my peace ended when my uncle moved in with us for a year. His abuse followed the same pattern as my grandfather's. Powerlessness left me defeated.

When my mother got married again, Husband #3 hated me like the others. Because money was tight, food scarcity was always a source of heated arguments. Padlocks on the refrigerator and cabinets kept my younger brother and me from taking food. My stomach never stopped grumbling.

"Can I have just a little more?" I asked one night at supper after finishing the small portion of meatless

FREEDOM STORIES

Hamburger Helper on my plate. Our main staple didn't satisfy my growing body. "I'm still hungry."

"We're all hungry," my stepfather growled. "Clear your plate, and get out of here."

I stomped to the sink. "I'm sick of it."

Anger flooded my stepdad. He threw back his chair and punched my eye, then boxed my face.

My mother didn't even flinch.

I snapped. "You're going to stand there and watch him hit me?"

I'd never confronted my mother, and she responded with silence. She walked into my room and filled a paper bag with my clothes.

"You need to find somewhere else to live." My mother's eyes were ice. "I'm going to make this marriage work."

I stumbled outside in disbelief. Sunlight made me squint, reminding me of the blow to my eye. Shock numbed me as I walked down the block in a daze. *Where would I go? What would I do?*

I was only 12.

❧❧❧

Staying with friends lasted only a few weeks before their parents started asking questions. I refused to return to foster care, so I scoped out the house of a friend of a friend. Divorce left the father living alone. The abandoned tree house in the backyard would make the perfect shelter.

54

WHY ME?

The set-up worked for longer than I'd imagined was possible.

The owner worked nights, so every morning I left after he headed to bed. On my way to school, I shoplifted a honeybun from a convenience store.

Gum was my toothpaste. Alternating stores kept me safe from suspicious managers. I hauled all my possessions in a gym bag.

At school, I ducked into the bathroom where I sponged myself with paper towels and liquid soap. During lunch, I hung out near the trash cans. Leftover food kept the hunger at bay. After school, I washed my clothes under the water from the backyard hose. Wet clothes dried in the tree house while I hung out until darkness forced me to sleep. Light would have given away my secret. Most nights, I lay on the hard floor, staring at the stars, wishing I had a real home and a family who loved me. Loneliness was my constant companion.

Thunderstorms made sleep difficult. When the weather was too bad to venture out of the neighborhood, I stole dog food from the neighbor's yard to eat.

I shopped for clothes in the lost and found at school. I rarely missed class or church. I forged school notes and made excuses for my parents' absence at conferences.

Curious people thought I came to church on my own since I no longer attended the same church as my grandmother.

During the summer, I found odd jobs pulling weeds and painting mailboxes. When I had enough money, I bought a mower at a flea market and started mowing yards. I hid the mower in a large drainage ditch. When it got stolen, I found another cheap mower to buy.

For a kid in special education classes, my resourcefulness gave me the courage to ask my teacher to retest me. I could do better. I wasn't an idiot. Repeating the third grade three times resulted from my early abuse, not my lack of intelligence.

My teacher agreed. "I've always believed in you, Ken. Let's spend some extra time on your studies. You can take the test at the end of the school year."

I tested out of "resource." I would enter high school without extra help.

The Christmas before my 15th birthday, my uncle showed up at Sunday school with a Christmas gift.

"Your mom said I'd probably find you here since she hasn't seen you," he explained. The confusion on my Sunday school teacher's face wasn't lost on me.

Inside the poorly wrapped package was a cheap razor. I mumbled my thanks, and my uncle took off. The visit was as strange as his gift.

After class, Miss Shelia stopped me, her eyebrows knit together in concern. "What did your uncle mean about your mom, Ken?"

I exhaled, grateful to finally share my secret.

Tears spilled down her face as I related my living conditions. The emotions I had stuffed for so long erupted in a torrent of grief.

"I'm so sorry, Ken." Miss Shelia grabbed me in a fierce

embrace. Sobs racked her body. "How could I be so out of tune with God that I didn't know this?"

Genuine love washed over me. Someone actually cared for me.

"I don't have much," she confided. "But I would've done anything to help you out if only I'd known." Miss Shelia squeezed my hands. "I'm so sorry, Ken."

I wanted to tell her not to blame herself, but the words wouldn't get past the lump in my throat.

"Come with me." She led me down the hall. "We need to talk with Pastor Mark."

Twenty minutes later, Pastor Mark shook his head in disbelief. "You're coming home with me. But first, we're getting some food in you."

An hour later, I could hardly grasp the turn of events. I sat in a booth with my pastor and his family at an all-you-can-eat restaurant. My plate held more food than I normally ate in an entire week.

❧❧❧

Pastor Mark contacted my mother the following week only to get an earful of accusations.

My hands shook. Things were about to get ugly. I'd run away before I'd go back to her house. But Pastor Mark's next words relieved my fears.

"Why didn't you file a missing child report?" He challenged the lies and refused to back down.

My mother hung up.

Pastor Mark patted my shoulder. "I'm sorry about your mother, Ken." Compassion filled his eyes. "You're welcome to stay here. Our home is yours."

Relief nearly buckled my legs under me.

Life with Pastor Mark, his wife, Melody, and their kids felt like a dream. I couldn't thank them enough for a warm bed, a real shower and three meals a day. They took me shopping for clothes and gave me a dresser to use. No longer did I have to haul my clothes around with me in a bag.

On weekends, we spent time together as a family — something I'd never experienced. I always thought restaurants were for rich people, so I especially loved eating out, even at the food court in the mall.

Pastor Mark thought I should attempt to reconnect with my mother. One overnight with her left me begging to come back. Pastor Mark and Melody readily agreed.

Six months later, Genevieve surprised me with a phone call. She'd married a military man, and they were living in Hawaii.

"We'd love for you to come live with us."

"Seriously?" I practically squealed over the phone. Starting a new life with my favorite person in the world was more than I could imagine. "That would be so awesome."

"Great. I'll purchase your ticket."

Pastor Mark was equally excited for me, but since he didn't have official custody of me, he contacted my mother for her consent.

WHY ME?

Anger spewed from her mouth. "If you go to Hawaii," she threatened me, "I'll file you as a runaway."

My disappointment was huge, especially when my mom told Genevieve lies that created a rift with her. But I couldn't risk getting sent back to foster care, not when Pastor Mark provided such a loving home.

Being older than my classmates proved challenging in high school. I made the track team, only to be dismissed once the coaches learned that I was too old to compete.

"Maybe you should consider a GED," Pastor Mark suggested. "You can work at the parsonage and start preparing for your future."

I agreed to his counsel.

෨෨෨

Summer brought a new experience for me — church camp. I loved the adventure of being outdoors, hanging out with friends and playing baseball and horseshoes. Though I didn't know it at the time, one of my best friends at camp, a girl three years younger than me, would later become my wife.

At the end of the summer, I loaded my bag into my Nissan pickup and hopped into the driver's seat, still on an emotional high from camp. The night before, I'd surrendered my future to God. Samuel, Pastor Mark's 8-year-old son, begged to sit next to the window, so my friend Fran scooted between us.

I hung the plate-sized gold medallion I'd won as

"Camp King" from the rearview mirror and followed Pastor Mark toward home. Excited kids waved to us from the back of his van. Wind rushed through the open windows of the pickup. The three of us jammed out to DC Talk. Life was good.

Around us, the summer's drought left its mark on the environment. I lost sight of Pastor Mark as dust devils swept over the land, twirling in little tornados. Soon we were the sole vehicle on a stretch of lonely highway.

"Time is Ticking Away" blared from the speakers when dirt swirled through my window. The wind hit the medallion, temporarily blinding me to the road in front of me. I swerved too fast and crossed the traffic lane.

I jerked the wheel and slid off the road. The Nissan flipped twice before finally resting. My heart pounded inside my chest. Everything had happened so fast.

"No! No! No!" Fran's screams pierced the air. She wrestled herself free of the windshield and stared into Samuel's face. "He's dead. He's dead. He's dead."

"Samuel?" I turned toward the boy I loved like a brother. A gash ran from his forehead to the bridge of his nose. A flap of skin folded back to reveal his skull. Blood suddenly spurted from the wound.

"Hold on, buddy!" I pulled his lifeless body through the passenger side window and started CPR. Fran didn't stop screaming.

We needed help. We were miles from the nearest town, stuck in a ditch out of sight of any cars that might pass and in an era long before the birth of cell phones. No one from home would turn back to look for us until he or she suspected something amiss.

Come on, buddy. I breathed into his mouth. *Dear God, please don't take him.*

A minute stretched into 10 before someone finally noticed the accident and called for an ambulance. The crunch of tires made me turn. Paramedics rushed toward us at the same time Pastor Mark arrived.

"Get him back!" I yelled to a bystander, but it was too late.

Pastor Mark stumbled toward Samuel, wailing in horror at the sight of his son. The sound was unbearable.

I staggered out of the way. Wide eyes stared in disbelief from the windows of the van. Kids cried for their parents.

The paramedics strapped Samuel's small frame onto the stretcher. The entire trip to the hospital, I begged God to spare him.

The waiting room was packed full of people when the doctor approached our group.

"Are you the one who was performing CPR?" he asked me. I could only nod.

"I regret to inform you that Samuel did not make it."

Pastor Mark stumbled toward me. "What did the doctor say?"

"Samuel's gone," I choked out.

He crumpled to the floor, his mournful cry haunting me.

It was my fault. It was all my fault.

FREEDOM STORIES

❧❧❧

Two hours later, a local church opened its doors for our group.

"Why, God?" I leaned against the gym wall and wailed. It wasn't fair. I'd emerged from the accident with only a bruised elbow and a cracked sternum. "Why didn't you take me, God? I should've died. Not him."

Samuel wanted to be just like his dad. The kid would play outside in his three-piece suit, then fall asleep still wearing the outfit. He was a born pastor.

Melody arrived at the church and found me. I waited for the blows I deserved. I killed the son of the people who had opened their home to me for two years.

Instead, she wrapped her arms around me in an embrace. "Let's get one thing right." She didn't mince her words. "I'm hurting. But I will never believe that you killed my son. Not now. Not until the day I die. I'll never hold you accountable."

Her words brought comfort, but a weight settled on me. I'd brushed against death one too many times. Why did God keep sparing me? Why didn't I have permanent brain damage after the repeated blows to my head? Why did God restore my sight? I even should have been paralyzed after a playground accident in elementary school. Why was I still walking around? *Why me, God?*

Samuel's death left a gnawing emptiness inside me. I joined an intern program at our church called the Master's Commission program. It was the least I could do to honor

WHY ME?

Samuel's life. The last night of summer camp, I'd prayed that God would use me. If I became a pastor, maybe then I'd understand why God kept me alive.

৵৵৵

I accepted a youth pastor position in Louisiana at the end of the Master's Commission program and met Gina. Life finally seemed full of promise. We married, then moved to Florida where I worked construction and volunteered as a youth pastor. Three years later, I accepted a position in Georgia where a pastor was starting a new church.

One Sunday morning, Gina and I argued before the church services. She wanted to wear a revealing outfit I didn't feel was appropriate, especially given my role. I left to play the drums, thinking she'd follow and we'd make up later. Gina never showed up at church. A sick feeling washed over me.

I drove to the home where she'd been taking art lessons and found Gina with her teacher. Turns out, they'd been having an affair.

"How could you?" I shook my head in disbelief. *Did our vows mean nothing?*

Cold eyes met mine. "We're through. I'm done with God and church."

Gina refused marriage counseling, so I resigned my position against the pastor's advice. *How could I help people when I couldn't even figure out my own life?* I refused to shave and only showered when the stench got too strong. I went through the motions in a construction job and retreated like a hermit after the work day ended. I lived off TV dinners and slept on the living room floor.

Betrayal opened wounds from my past. People and intimacy scared me.

Six months later, a divorced lady from church called. As soon as she arrived at my house, I had a bad feeling. While I pondered what to do, the doorbell rang.

"Don't do it," a guy on my doorstop blurted out. "God sent me to tell you, 'Don't do it.'"

My jaw dropped open when I recognized him. I'd met the man two years earlier at a pastors' conference in Florida. We'd sat at the same table, a brief encounter of two random people in a crowd of attendees.

"How'd you find me?" I stuttered in disbelief.

The guy shrugged. "I've been driving all day. God brought me to your address."

Dumbfounded, I invited him inside. I didn't even know the guy's name.

The woman left when her objective failed, and I dropped to my knees.

"God, I'm so sorry for giving up on life." The words poured from my heart. I was desperate to feel his presence again. "I'm a wreck. I need you. Please forgive me."

The next day, I noticed the sunrise for the first time in months. I knew then that I needed to be purposeful about my relationships. I couldn't do life alone. I needed to intentionally pursue godly relationships.

WHY ME?

❧ ❧ ❧

I punched in the long-distance number on my phone. It had been too long since I'd connected with Ann, my best friend from summer camp years before.

"Pastor Jones?" I cleared my throat when Ann's father answered the phone. "This is Ken."

Surprise flooded his voice. "Ken, it's been too long. How are you?"

After catching up, I asked him for Ann's number. He looked through the contacts on his cell phone and accidentally dialed her number.

"Nice to hear from you, Ken." He gave Ann my number and hung up. She called me right back.

Hearing Ann's voice brought back a wave of good memories.

Ann and I talked for more than an hour. I'd missed our friendship more than I'd realized.

Ann had fled an abusive relationship two years earlier, and she and her 4-year-old daughter, Ansley, were living in Dallas. Just when I was ready to give up on life, I fell headlong in love.

Six months later, the two of us got married.

Life with Ann was a fresh start. Our friendship laid a foundation for our love. I adored Ansley and couldn't wait until Ann and I had more children.

I started my own landscape company so I could provide for my family. I vowed to be the father I never had.

৵৵৵

A siren wailed, breaking my stream of memories. *Was I hallucinating? Had I died?*

People rushed toward me. The sight of the ambulance brought hope.

A tumble of words stopped at my mouth. My silence was maddening. I could hear every conversation around me, but I was powerless to speak.

"Get me something to dig him out!" a paramedic yelled. "The concrete's hardening."

A flurry of movement blurred before me.

A burly paramedic pounded the concrete. My teeth vibrated with the force. A large chunk broke loose. Then another, breaking the pressure on my head.

"He's free!" someone shouted. "Get the stretcher."

Strong hands lifted me onto the gurney, while a paramedic fitted an oxygen mask over my mouth and nose. I gulped in air. The ambulance rushed me to the hospital.

The sight of my wife at the hospital made my heart soar.

"Babe, I'm right here," Ann told me. My silence made the lines in her forehead crease.

"Will he be brain dead?" she asked the doctor as I was unloaded off the gurney and onto a bed in the emergency room.

The doctor couldn't answer without running tests. His silence terrified me.

WHY ME?

In the emergency room, the nurses peeled dried concrete off my face. With only carbon dioxide to feed my cells, my body had started shutting down. An hour later and I would have been dead.

"I thought we lost you." Ann gripped my hand. "I don't know what I would've done without you."

I closed my eyes and breathed a prayer of gratitude. I was so thankful that Ann had known I was in trouble, even though I couldn't speak. I was even more grateful that she thought to have AT&T ping my cell phone to determine my location.

Four days later, I walked out of the hospital in perfect health.

৵৵৵

I started to fear working alone. The idea of running my own business again terrified me.

What if I couldn't provide for my family?

I closed my business and worked for another contractor, while Ann and I compiled a wish list. The time seemed right for me to resume full-time ministry.

An opportunity to become a pastor opened in San Antonio. My dream quickly became my worst nightmare.

How could I have been so wrong? I asked God. *Don't you want me to be a pastor?*

Wanting a fresh start, Ann and I moved to Round Rock where we quickly connected at Freedom Church. I took a job working for another construction company.

FREEDOM STORIES

Our second Sunday at Freedom Church, Pastor Benito preached a message about God using all of our life experiences. A flood of pain hit me as I thought about Samuel.

Still searching for meaning in all the fragmented pieces of my past, I went forward to pray at the altar. Pastor Ben met me on my knees.

Please, God, show me that my pain has not been for nothing.

ঝঝঝ

It would be three years before I realized that God had a totally radical plan for my life. Through Pastor Benito's preaching, I realized that I needed to stop living in the past, daily reliving and regretting what had happened to Samuel. I realized that no matter what I had been through or what I was going through, I needed to pursue what God had for my life.

Surrendering to God didn't mean I had to serve behind a pulpit. I could use my talents to build a business where I hired men struggling to find work. While my employees rebuilt houses, God could rebuild lives.

I thought back to doctors' predictions that I would be sterile after a childhood accident. Like the seed which birthed my two daughters, God was planting a seed in me to birth this new business.

God had defied the odds in my life. He'd do the same again.

WHY ME?

I got excited sharing the dream with Ann. My heart leapt while we imagined the possibilities. "Just think about it. Every year, we could go on a mission trip together as a team."

Ann embraced the idea, and we launched our construction business. Our mission to rebuild lives is based on God's promise to make all things new in Christ Jesus. This year we've committed to join a Belize missions team. We'll be working alongside a ministry dedicated to helping women and children escape sex trafficking.

When I agreed to share my story in *Freedom Stories*, Pastor Benito gave me a huge hug.

"Remember when you came to the altar three years ago?"

I was surprised that he remembered.

"God didn't forget. Your pain won't be for nothing."

I nodded slowly, thinking of my interview with the writer. I knew exactly where I'd begin. Where it all nearly ended.

Tick, tick, tick.

Time taunted me.

Every second drove me to work like a madman. I pressed my limits in a rush against the clock.

The heat index pushed the temperature to 111 degrees. Sunrays bathed the concrete around me, hardening the wet grey mix into white stone …

RESCUED
The Story of Sylvia
Written by Karen Koczwara

"He said he wants to sleep with me," I told my stepfather, feeling sick at saying the words out loud. I waited for him to react, to spew with anger in my defense. But instead, he simply shrugged off my words.

"Oh, men will be men," my stepfather said coolly. "Sometimes they just say stuff like that."

Didn't you hear what I said? Don't you care? A married man made advances on a teenage girl! Doesn't that sicken you as much as it sickens me?

But my stepfather didn't seem to care.

My blood boiled. *You know what? I'm done with you. I'm done with all of you!* I reeled, remembering the times men had taken advantage of me despite my protests. I didn't tell anyone, because I didn't think anyone would believe me. And it was probably just as well. *No one takes me seriously.*

I'll just live my own life from now on! Screw all of you! I'm going to do what I want. I don't care how reckless things get.

Let the fun begin!

෨෨෨

I was born in Dallas, Texas. My parents divorced before I reached my first birthday. My father suffered from a mental illness and became aggressive with my mother during her pregnancy with me. My mother met a new man shortly after the divorce, and they married when I was 2. That man became my dad, and I rarely saw my biological father after that. My mother and stepfather had a child together, and my new sister and I grew especially close. But the cycle of dysfunction soon set in again.

My stepfather, a supervisor for a cabinet company, was a hard worker and wonderful provider. However, he was physically and verbally abusive at home. If my sister and I produced good grades, he praised us. If we brought home a less-than-ideal grade, however, he grew angry and beat us. On more than one occasion, he flew into a rage and flipped over the dining table, forcing my sister and me to jump out of the way. We grew afraid of his unpredictable behavior, never knowing what sort of mood he'd be in at the end of the day.

When I turned 8, my parents bought my aunt's ranch in San Antonio. With ample trees and sprawling land, the place was a young child's paradise. My cousins lived nearby, and we enjoyed playing outside with them. When the sun sank behind the trees and my stepfather's truck rounded the bend, we hopped in the back of the truck and bounced up and down as he drove the rest of the way home. But behind closed doors, the tension in our home grew. My stepfather struggled to find a job making the equivalent pay he'd earned in Dallas, and financial pressures mounted. He lost his temper at even the smallest things. My mother took a job at a bank and often came home past our bedtime. My stepfather sat in the dark, fuming as he waited for her to show up.

"You're cheating, aren't you?" he accused, his angry words flying down the hall where my sister and I tried to sleep. "That bank closed hours ago, and it's almost 11 p.m.! Where the h*** you been, huh?"

"I'm not cheating!" my mother retorted, but I wondered if she was.

As the fighting continued and my parents' marriage began to self-destruct, I longed for Dallas, where life had seemed simpler and happier. "I want things back the old way," I lamented to my sister.

On Sundays, my parents took us to a little Catholic church in San Antonio. Being Hispanic, attending the Catholic Church seemed the proper thing to do. We went through the rituals, and my mother, often bored, sometimes scrawled a grocery list in her seat while the priest spoke. She and my stepfather gave money faithfully, reminding me that it was important to help the church. I learned about God there, but I didn't really understand his role in my life. My mother often threatened that God would punish me if I misbehaved. I began to see him as an angry guy in the sky, much like my angry stepfather at home. I partook in all the expected steps — Catechism, communion and confession — but they didn't make much sense to me. I still had many questions.

"Why do I have to do confession before communion?"

I asked my mother. "Why can't I just talk to God directly?"

No one seemed to have convincing answers. I'd always had a strong sense of right and wrong, and deep down, I desired to know God more. But I wasn't sure throwing a few bucks in the plate or confessing my wrongdoings before communion was going to bring me any closer to God.

When I turned 11, my parents divorced. My stepfather returned to Dallas, and my mother stayed with us in San Antonio. I was both sad and relieved. I would not miss the fighting, but still, we had been a family, and now our family was torn in two. My parents used my sister and me like chess pawns, playing games with each other as we bounced back and forth between their homes.

"Don't tell your mom what I'm doing," my stepfather threatened. My mother, in turn, tried being sneaky with him. Neither of them wanted the other to know what they were doing with their single lives. Mom's temper grew worse, and she often spanked me in anger. I became confused and hurt, again longing for the days of stability.

One day, my mother announced she and my stepfather were getting back together. We packed up and moved into his little condo in Irving, just outside Dallas. Just as we settled in, the fighting escalated. On my stepfather's birthday, my mother announced she was moving my sister and me back to San Antonio for good.

"How could you do this to him on his birthday?" I cried, enraged at her insensitivity.

RESCUED

My mother slapped me across the face. "You don't talk back to me!" she snapped.

The chess game continued. My sister and I became victims of their game, forced to continually switch schools as they struggled to make up their minds. My parents reunited and remarried, but after just a short while, they divorced again. My mother moved us into a rundown four-plex in San Antonio and headed out to nightclubs after we went to bed. My sister and I huddled in our beds, hoping the deadbolt on the door did its job. Often, my mother brought company back to the house, and we covered our ears as strange noises wafted from the other room.

"You can't leave those girls alone! They are too young!" my stepfather reprimanded her when he learned of my mother's careless ways.

But my mother didn't care. She was enjoying her freedom. Sometimes, I welcomed her being gone, as it meant she wouldn't yell at us. Other times, I longed for her presence. *I just want her to be a mom. I want her back.*

A lady across the way noticed our plight, and she invited us to spend time with her during the day. My aunts and cousins nearby also cared for us when my mother disappeared. They grew angry with my mother's behavior as well.

"You need to take care of those kids!" they cried.

But my mother didn't listen.

She often dropped my sister and me off at a friend's house, and we spent the night there when my mother dashed off to the clubs. One night, the lady's husband slipped into the room as we slept and began to touch me inappropriately. I cringed in the dark, feeling sick. Relief washed over me when he slipped back out of the room. I considered telling my mother, but I knew she wouldn't believe me. At last, she stopped taking us over there, and I was glad.

We visited my stepfather often, and his cousin tried to touch me one night, too. Again, I kept the terrible secret to myself. I felt sick to my stomach, wondering why God would not help me. *I'm not a bad kid, God! Are you trying to punish me for something, like my mother said? Why won't you come to my rescue and pull me out of this nightmare?*

The more unstable life became, the angrier I grew. I began hanging out with a married couple in our four-plex, and they treated me nicely. Though I was just 11 and they were in their late 20s, they offered me weed. Wanting to be numb, I grabbed the joint and took a long hit. I loved the way my problems melted away as the pot sank into my lungs. *So this is what it means to escape. I could get used to this.*

I went back home and took a bath to wash off the smell. But I knew I'd be back for more.

I continued smoking weed every chance I could. Many of my family members smoked it, too, and gaining access to the drug was never a problem. Often, we took a few swigs of the booze they left lying around, too. I no longer cared about life. I simply wanted to escape the pain, instability and confusion. Thoughts of death crept in, and I wondered what it might be like to float away from this hell on earth. But then I thought of my little sister, whom I felt especially responsible for. I loved her and would be crushed if anything happened to her. I would stay alive for her.

One day, my mother brought home a nice man. He treated my sister and me well, and I was happy my mother had found someone nice at last. At school, I drew a picture and gave it to him.

"Are you going to put it on your fridge?" I asked, my eyes hopeful.

But a few days later, I saw the picture lying around our house.

"Why didn't he take it home with him?" I asked my mother, my heart filling with disappointment.

She gave a tight-lipped smile. "Because he is married."

My blood boiled. "You are dating a guy who's married? You can't be with a guy who's married!" I couldn't believe it. Prince Charming was too good to be true after all. *I've had it with both of them! This is crazy!*

But my mother continued to date the married man. One day, he got physically violent, grabbing her by the hair as she yelped in protest.

"If you don't let her go, I'm gonna call the cops!" I screamed.

He finally released his grip.

"Why are you letting this guy treat you that way?" I said to my mother in disgust. I stormed off to my room and cried. I had no one to talk to about the situation. I could not tell the rest of my family because they were already fed up with my mother's irresponsible behavior. I cried out to God. *Why won't you rescue me from all of this? Where are you?*

When I turned 13, my sister and I went to live with my stepfather back in Dallas. His place became a refuge, a haven in my bleak world. He provided the stability we'd been longing for. I didn't worry about his rages anymore. His temper seemed to have lessened. Often, he picked us up for lunch and took us back to his work, where we busied ourselves making copies in the office. We attended sporting events on the weekends and enjoyed normalcy for the first time in a very long while. But that momentary peace was soon threatened again.

One night, my stepfather dropped me off at his older daughter's house. Several years my senior, she was married and had a baby of her own. She asked me to go to the store with her husband, and I agreed. As he and I sat in the car, he pulled out a joint, and we got high together.

"I've noticed your body has been changing," he said, giving me a once-over from his seat. "You are turning into a really beautiful young girl."

The sick feeling in my stomach returned, this time with a punch. *No, no. Please, not again.*

"I want to be with you, Sylvia," he continued. "I know you're a virgin, and it would be best for you to let me take your virginity from you."

I immediately felt sick.

RESCUED

How can he be saying this stuff? Is this really happening to me?

I remained speechless, wanting to scratch his face or punch him in the throat. He didn't say another word, and we continued on home.

I tossed and turned on their couch that night, afraid to fall asleep for fear he would sneak in and try to touch me. *No one will believe me if he does,* I realized with a sinking feeling. *No one will rescue me.*

One night, his wife fell asleep on the couch in the living room. I heard the baby crying in his bassinet in her bedroom, and I slipped into the room to check on him. I sat on the edge of the bed and patted the baby to soothe him, while her husband slept a few feet away. Suddenly, she stormed into the room.

"What are you doing in here? Trying to sleep with my husband?" she accused angrily.

"No!" I cried, jumping up. "Miles was crying, and I was just trying to calm him!" I fled the room, ashamed and upset. *How dare she accuse me of trying to make moves on her husband? If only she knew what he'd said to me!*

Unable to keep it in any longer, I told my stepfather what her husband had said. "He told me he wants to sleep with me!" I said breathlessly, expecting my stepfather to grow angry.

But instead, my stepfather simply brushed it off. "Oh, men will be men," he said coolly. "Sometimes they just say stuff like that."

A new kind of anger boiled inside. *I'm done with all of you! I am gonna go live my life the way I want to, whether you like it or not!*

I threw myself into every possible rebellious act, cranking up heavy metal music, doing drugs, vandalizing property and even learning about witchcraft. *Anything that makes me feel powerful over my powerless life.* If someone at school looked at me the wrong way, I went off on him or her. I was an angry wrecking ball of hurt, ready to plow down anyone in my path.

I began high school in Irving. I began taking LSD, dropping acid with my friends every day before class. Cocaine and meth soon followed. We hung out at a convenience store across from school, waiting for the dealers to arrive. I didn't care what drug I did, just as long as I remained numb. I didn't want to feel anything or face the pain.

Though I wanted to do well in school, my grades plummeted from A's and B's to C's and D's. I met a boy who seemed to love me. I tried to get clean for a few months and pulled up my grades.

At school, all the kids talked about their future and which colleges they planned to attend. I wanted to make my life better. But, as a wounded soul wanting to be rescued, I tried finding security in my troubled boyfriend instead.

"I'm running away to live with my mom in Dallas," my boyfriend announced. "You should go with me."

I contemplated the idea. Running away sounded nice.

RESCUED

An escape from reality, a chance to start over. Meanwhile, my stepfather threatened to put me in rehab.

"I'm not doing drugs anymore," I tried to convince him. But he didn't believe me. He thought he knew best.

"My dad wants to put me in rehab," I told my boyfriend, rolling my eyes.

"Let me ask my mom if you can come live with us." He returned with some good news. His mother had an extra bed. I could leave with him right away.

And so I did just that. I ran away from home without telling a soul. I thought of my younger sister, feeling terrible for leaving her behind.

I hoped she'd be okay, but I couldn't stick around and wallow in my troubles for the rest of my life. I was now nearly 16 and believed I was old enough to make decisions for myself.

After settling in with my boyfriend, I eventually contacted my stepfather and sister. They were both very hurt and angry.

"You can't come back home," my stepfather insisted. "You're on your own now."

His words stung, but I didn't care. My sister shared her hurts as well, but I tried to brush them off. *I'm tired of everything in my life. It's time to live the way I want to.*

I quit school and continued living with my boyfriend. He became physically and verbally abusive, but I put up with his behavior. *I've been knocked around my whole life. This is just the way men are. Just gotta suck it up.* I convinced myself I loved him, that beneath his tough exterior lay a guy who truly loved me back. Perhaps we could create a happily ever after together.

I became pregnant at 16. Juan struggled to hold down a job, and we lived with his mother while surviving on food stamps and welfare. I knew this was no way to bring a child into the world, but I was determined to keep the baby and make things work. I remained in the relationship, convinced I could change him, convinced I would someday be enough for him.

As the abuse and fighting continued, I finally made up my mind to leave him. But when Juan learned of my plan, he grew distraught, threw himself on the floor and stuck a gun to his head. "If you walk out those doors, the last thing you'll hear is this gun going off," he threatened.

I recoiled, sick to my stomach at the thought of Juan killing himself. Instead of leaving, I stayed.

I gave birth to a little girl, Sandra, and just 13 months later, I gave birth again, this time to a little boy, Edgar. Juan's abuse escalated, and he began lying to me and pursuing other women. I continued with reckless behavior of my own, and we fought regularly. *I'll change him someday,* I told myself.

"You don't deserve this sort of life," a friend said, pulling me aside one day. "You need to get out."

At last, I knew what I had to do, no matter what consequences ensued. Juan and I were a ticking time bomb waiting to explode. But how could I leave after having two children with him? And what if he really did change one day?

RESCUED

I called my stepdad and told him I planned to leave Juan. He agreed to help me get back on my feet. "Come home, and I'll help you," he promised.

I packed the kids' diaper bags but took nothing else. My stepfather pulled up, and I grabbed the kids, by then ages 3 and 2, and walked out the door. Juan and his buddies sat in the front yard, drunk on whiskey. As I placed the kids into the car, he cussed and screamed at me. My stepfather climbed out of the car with his rifle, afraid Juan might try to harm me.

I whirled around and faced Juan, summoning all the strength in my body. "I am not coming back," I said firmly. "We're done."

Juan continued to spew threatening words, but I no longer cared. *I don't want to live like this anymore. I am done. I can never fix this guy, and I know that now for sure.*

I returned to Irving with my stepfather, and he gave up his room for me and the kids. Though happy to reunite with my sister, I had no idea what to do with the rest of my life. I landed two jobs and put the kids in daycare. My stepfather picked the kids up after work, and I was grateful for his help. Though our early days together had been rocky, he had eventually proven himself the more stable parent.

Despite working two jobs, money remained tight. Juan called often, lamenting how much he missed me. "Come back. We can be a family again," he tried to convince me.

I took a deep breath, so badly wanting to believe we

could. But I remembered his patterns, his destructive ways. *Empty promises,* I reminded myself. *You can't trust this guy.*

Still, I let Juan visit the kids when he could. One day, after returning from work, I received a phone call from him. "You are not getting your kids back," he threatened. "And if you try to come get them, I'll kill you."

My body weakened, and I feared I might collapse. *My babies! No!*

I took the threat seriously, sure that if I showed up at Juan's door, he'd murder me. I'd have to comply with him. Calling the police was too dangerous, and if I told my stepfather, he'd probably murder Juan himself. I'd have to keep the terrible secret to myself.

"When are the kids coming back?" my stepfather asked.

"It's too hard holding down two jobs and trying to pay for daycare on my own," I told him, my heart thudding with every word of my lie. "I let Juan have them until I get back on my feet."

I threw myself into the party scene, going out to clubs at night, drinking and dancing. I tried not to think about my children, as it was too painful. *Please, God, don't let him hurt them. Please let them be okay.*

One day, my mother came for a visit. "Where are those kids? I want to see how much they've grown," she said.

I sucked in my breath and decided to tell her the truth. "Mom, Juan threatened me. He took them and said he'd kill me if I tried to get them back."

RESCUED

"Those are your kids, Sylvia!" my mother cried. "You need to call the police right now!"

My stomach lurched. I didn't want to get the police involved. But with no official custody agreement, did I stand a chance of getting my kids back on my own?

I called Juan and demanded to see my kids.

"If you wanna see your kids, you gotta sleep with me," he retorted.

My skin crawled at the idea. But I was desperate. "Fine," I agreed.

I arrived at Juan's grandmother's house, where he insisted I meet him. He let me have the kids, and I pretended to take him back, saying and doing all the right things to appease him. I then drove back to my stepfather's house, pleased with myself for duping him.

"We need to move right away," I told my stepfather. "If Juan finds us, he'll threaten me again."

We moved, and I tried to resume life as a single mother. Realizing it was too difficult to work and pay for childcare, I opted to stay home and live off of food stamps and welfare for the time being. Eventually, I landed a job at a grocery store. I met a new guy and got pregnant. I kept the secret to myself, knowing my stepfather would not react well to the news. *If you get pregnant again, I'll put you out,* he'd once said. I couldn't afford to live on my own, so I'd have to keep things under wraps.

My new guy led a troubled life, and I knew I didn't want to be with him. I hid my pregnancy behind large tunic shirts and focused on work. I struck up a friendship with the assistant manager at the grocery store and enjoyed his company. Harvey, several years my senior, was a friendly and caring man who took a genuine interest in me. When his wife, four months pregnant, was struck and killed by a drunk driver, my heart broke for him. I wanted to reach out and show him I cared, but I had my own set of troubles.

After a few weeks, my manager returned to work. I expressed my condolences, and he asked me to hang out. By now, my stomach had grown so much I could no longer hide it. I imagined how he must feel, having just lost both his wife and unborn child. I gave birth to a little boy, and we continued hanging out. Things between us felt natural, and I developed strong feelings for him. But something in my heart held me back. I didn't feel he had fully mourned his wife and knew he needed time to absorb the tragedy.

"We need to take a break," I said. "Just until you're 100 percent sure you're ready to move on."

Harvey reluctantly agreed. Several months later, he returned with words I welcomed. "I know what I want. And I don't want to live without you."

Harvey and I married the following year and moved into a house together. For the first time in my life, I'd met someone who treated me with respect. Harvey had grown up in a Christian home and had never touched drugs. When I told him about my past, he didn't judge me, but instead listened with an open heart.

"You know I love you just the way you are, Sylvia," he

told me sweetly. "I don't care what you've done in your past."

Relief swept over me at his words. *Safe and secure at last! Harvey is a real man!*

Though Harvey and I didn't go to church, he had a Bible, and I tried to read it. I was still unsure what I thought of God after all these years. I was still pretty sure he was an angry guy in the sky, ready to punish me if I messed up. Church seemed like a place full of strange, boring rituals. In my darkest times, I'd cried out to God, pleading with him to rescue me. He hadn't rescued me, but instead, I'd suffered great pain. I felt sure that the God of the Bible didn't really care about a messed-up girl like me.

Harvey's parents, devout Christians, tried to share their understanding of God with me. I remained polite but internally brushed them off. *You don't know what I've been through. Easy for you to talk about this loving God, but I've been through hell.*

I gave birth once more, this time to another little boy weighing a whopping 11 pounds, 6 ounces. After such a difficult birth, I decided I was done having children. Our family was complete.

My emotional issues began to catch up with me. I knew I needed to deal with my past, but it seemed too painful to revisit. I grew depressed and often withdrew from Harvey and my children. Anxiety attacks plagued me frequently. On several occasions, I feared I was dying.

"I love you," I told the kids, wrapping them in a long

hug. I was afraid it might be our last embrace, that our moments together might be few. Surely, I was going to die.

At last, I went to counseling. "I don't want to be angry anymore," I told the counselor. "I know I need help."

I opened up, sharing every detail of my past. Everything from the physical, sexual and emotional abuse rose to the surface. It felt freeing to address issues that had plagued me for so long. I began taking antidepressants, and the depression slowly lifted. As I grew comfortable sharing my story with the counselor, I realized I needed to put everything out in the open with Harvey as well. I'd told him the majority of my story, but there were still things he did not know. He was my husband, and I loved him and wanted our relationship to work. In order to move forward together, I needed to reveal the full truth.

Harvey remained positive and supportive. I was so grateful to have found such a wonderful man, so different than the guys in my past. Harvey truly loved me and my children, and I did not take his love for granted.

My biological father tried to contact me periodically over the years, but I did not welcome his attempts. He was mentally ill and verbally abusive and spewed hurtful words like, "You're fat just like your grandma." At last, I firmly told him I didn't want to communicate anymore. I was happily moving forward to a better place in life and preferred to leave all toxic relationships in the past.

Harvey and I bought a house in Garland, Texas. One day, the police showed up at the door. "You've been reported missing," they said after identifying me.

RESCUED

"By who?" My mind raced. All of my family members knew where I was. Was this some sort of joke?

"Your father is in the hospital after suffering a heart attack," the police explained. "Your biological sister reported you missing."

My biological sister? I had no relationship with her, but surely she could have just called around or looked me up online instead of reporting me missing! Something felt very fishy about the whole thing.

I drove to nearby Mesquite, where my father lay in the hospital. There, the doctors informed me he had a bleeding ulcer, which had presumably caused his heart attack. He was not doing well and would most likely not recover.

I met with my sister, who seemed to suffer from a mental illness of her own. She explained she had power of attorney and remained very dramatic about the entire situation. *How have I gotten myself in the middle of all this? And what am I supposed to do now?*

For the next couple weeks, my entire world stopped. My friend watched the kids while I spent time at the hospital, sitting with my biological father and sister. He took a turn for the worse and became extremely agitated. The doctors put him into an induced coma, and after a few days, they announced he seemed to be getting better. I still wasn't sure what I thought of this man who'd vanished from my life when I was a child, then belittled me with his words over the years. *I'm here out of obligation, but that's it.*

One evening, I wandered into his hospital room and found him sitting up in bed. "You're awake!" I exclaimed, shocked to see his eyes open.

"Sit down, Sylvia," he said with a smile. "You know what? I'm ready to go to heaven and be with Grandma." He then looked me straight in the eye. "I'm very sorry for how I've treated you over the years. I really love you, and I'm so sorry."

His kind words shocked me. I'd never seen my father so softened and humbled. "I forgive you, Dad. I really do."

"When I get out of here, we'll talk more," he assured me.

"Sounds good. I'll see you tomorrow."

I left late that night, perplexed by our encounter. *Did I really just have that conversation with my father, the guy who's called me fat my whole life? He seems so different, so at peace. But he doesn't look like a dying man. I think he's going to pull through.*

Around 3 a.m., the hospital called and asked me to come right away. When I arrived, the doctors told me my father had passed away.

"We had him in an induced coma, but we could not cauterize his bleeding ulcers, and he continued bleeding internally," they said somberly. "He suffered a massive heart attack."

"That's impossible!" I cried. "He was sitting up and talking to me earlier!"

The doctors stared at me, wide-eyed. I stared back at them in shock, replaying the conversation with my father over and over in my mind. *How can he be dead? I thought he was going to get better!*

I called my sister, and she freaked out at the news. We attempted to make funeral arrangements with what little resources we had. We then went to his apartment to sort through his stuff. As we went through piles of junk, I quickly realized two things: My father was a hoarder, and he liked guns. Suddenly, I realized how very little I knew of this man, and I felt sad. I wondered what my life would have been like if he had raised me, if we had really gotten acquainted with one another. Would there have been less pain or more?

"Look at this money order for $500!" My sister held up an old piece of paper. "If this is good, maybe we could use it to pay for the funeral."

Sometime later, my sister brought me another piece of paper. My stomach lurched as I read it. "A letter to Mom's attorney, giving up his personal rights to me," I croaked, shaking my head in disbelief. I imagined my father signing the letter. *Did you cry, Dad? Did you care? Or did you casually give me up with no intent to see me again?*

We contacted my father's family in Arkansas and made the trip back there to bury him. My sister, riddled by anxiety, popped Xanax and drank one beer after another. I grew anxious, too, and took my antidepressants to cope. Neither of us was prepared for such a whirlwind of events, and we hardly knew what to do with ourselves or this man we both called father.

During the funeral, I stared at the church bulletin with

my father's photo on it. The summary of his life stated that he had attended a Baptist church. *Huh. That's interesting. I never knew that.* Suddenly, my mind drifted to the idea of eternity. *Where did my father go when he died? Is he in heaven? How do you even make sure you go to heaven?* I'd read only bits and pieces of the Bible over the years and still wasn't sure what to make of everything. But suddenly, I wanted to know more. *Where was I going to go when I died?*

I returned to Texas and resumed life with my family. But the questions of eternity still nagged at me. One day, a couple of moms from my son's classroom invited me to their church.

"No, thanks," I said politely. "Organized religion isn't really my thing."

But they remained persistent. "We need help with our Vacation Bible School program. Are you willing to volunteer in the nursery?"

I hesitated, then agreed to do the job. To my surprise, I enjoyed it more than I'd anticipated. I began connecting with the women and sent my kids to the children's programs on Wednesday nights.

Though I cussed regularly and often had a bad attitude, the women remained kind and encouraging. They gently continued to ask me if I'd like to try out their church. At last, I agreed to go.

The church was much livelier than the Catholic church I'd attended as a kid. I sat up in the balcony way in the back where no one would bother me. *I'll just keep to myself and observe from afar,* I decided. A man always went out of his way to hug me and welcome me, however, and I appreciated his initiative. *Wow, these people are really nice here. Maybe this isn't so scary after all.*

One Sunday, the pastor announced a guest speaker would be addressing the audience in place of the three church services that day. I started to leave, but something held me back in my seat. The guest speaker stepped to the front and began to speak about spiritual warfare. I had never heard the term before, but as he talked, it started to make sense. He explained that God had an enemy, Satan, who tried everything in his power to defeat us. While God wanted to bring us life, both in eternity and on earth, Satan's primary goal was to destroy us emotionally, physically and spiritually. Satan was sneaky and would often try certain tactics to lure us in. On the outside, his tactics seemed desirable. But they were really destructive.

I shuddered as the man spoke, thinking of the few times I'd dabbled with witchcraft. *Is this the sort of stuff he's talking about? Was Satan messing with me?*

The man then discussed forgiveness. "We all have sin in our lives," he explained. "Sin is the wrong things we've done. We have wronged people, and we have been wronged by others as well." He then made a list of several common sins. I shuddered again, realizing I'd committed every offense he mentioned. *Wow. I've never really thought about this before.*

"The good news is, no matter how many offenses we've committed, it's never too late with God. He is ready to forgive, ready to embrace us with open arms if we ask him to cleanse us. You can do that today," the speaker concluded.

I sobbed, recalling the many wrong things I'd done. *If only people knew how bad I really was. Years ago, I robbed homes and vandalized property. I am a thief and a liar.*

As I made my mental list, I grew sick, remembering how many people I'd wronged in the midst of my anger and pain. Could God forgive a broken girl like me? This man insisted nothing was too great for God to handle. Was this really true?

For the first time in my life, I fully cried out to God. *God, why did it take you so long to get to me?*

And then, for the first time in my life, it was as if I heard him speak to me in my heart. *I have always been there, Sylvia. I was just waiting for you to come to me.*

Oh, God, really? The tears flowed freely as I replayed the words in my mind. I thought of the hurting little girl in that rundown four-plex, crying out to God in the midst of abuse. *Why didn't you rescue me, God?* I'd wondered then. But God had been there all along! Now I truly understood it. He had seen me and protected me, even in the darkest times. He had never left me alone.

I am sorry, God! I never realized how much I hurt you! And to think you were there for me all along! Suddenly, I had an overflowing sensation of being forgiven. Gratitude filled my heart, and I felt as if I might burst from emotion. *I believe God forgives me and loves me. I get it now. What a wonderful feeling to know he hasn't given up on me!*

The speaker asked us to make a list of those we needed to forgive. I thought of my parents, of Juan and of the men who had molested me when I was young. *I forgive them, God. You have forgiven me, and I know you want to forgive these people, too.* As I released my hurts to God, I felt the burdens being lifted. *What a relief! I don't have to carry this around anymore. I can be free!*

That day, I realized that Jesus loved me. And that day, I gave my heart to him. I walked out of there, knowing I'd never be the same again. I was loved, and I was forgiven. I was not alone, and I never had been. God had seen me in the darkness. All the bondage that had weighed me down for so long was gone, replaced by an unmistakable joy and peace. *I am a new person now! And, oh, how good it feels!*

I began attending church regularly and thanked God for bringing those wonderful women into my life. *I was a little rough around the edges, and they didn't give up on me. You put people in my life who loved me when I was unlovable. Thank you, God!*

Harvey joined me in my excitement about our new church. He had always had a relationship with God, but he was ready to dive in and give back now. Our pastor and his wife lovingly encouraged us to get involved. Harvey began helping with the children's ministry, and I lent a hand as well. Suddenly, we had another family — a place to belong and call home.

On Easter Sunday in 2007, my pastor shared my story

with the congregation, telling them what God had done in my life. He then invited me onto the stage. It was the first time my story had been shared publically, and God gave me the strength to be vulnerable. *Use my story to help someone else, God,* I prayed. *Help them to see how much you love them.*

Not long after, our youth pastors, Benito and Jennifer, moved, and I missed them terribly.

In 2008, I got a routine mammogram as part of my annual checkup after learning my insurance covered the procedure. When the church announced it would be taking a mission trip, I jumped on board. I was eager to do anything I could to share God's love with others. I embarked on an exciting trip to Honduras. While there, the doctor called and said he'd reviewed my mammogram and found something suspicious. I would soon find out that there were precancerous cells in my left breast.

Instead of panicking, I felt only peace. *God, you've already carried me through so much. I know you'll get me through this, too.*

I underwent two surgeries, and the doctors declared me cancer-free. *Thank you, God, for healing me!*

The whirlwind year continued. Harvey's truck, which he used for his landscaping business, was stolen and then mysteriously returned. Shortly after, I learned Juan had been shot and killed while robbing someone's house. I felt sick, thinking of my children's biological father's life ending so tragically. *He never changed,* I realized sadly. *And now he's gone forever.*

RESCUED

I sank into a depression as I grieved Juan. Though our relationship had been tumultuous, I still cared for him as a person and wished he had discovered God's love, too. *Oh, God, why did you save me and not him?*

I started to feel stuck again. The old feelings of depression returned, and I began crying out to God, asking him to answer some of the toughest questions of life.

Juan had had other children, and those boys were headed down a terrible path. They asked to live with me, but I knew I could not take them in. I could only be a place of encouragement and pray for them. *They're going to end up just like their father,* I feared, feeling helpless.

A deacon at our church, who had become like a father figure to me, recognized my slump and pulled me aside. "Sylvia, the enemy is using your passion for lost people against you. Don't let him do that. I know you're grieving Juan and wondering about his eternal fate. Everyone has a choice, and you chose to be obedient to the call of God. Pray that Juan's boys obey that call, too, someday."

He's right, I realized. I remembered the speaker's talk on spiritual warfare, and suddenly, it all made sense. I was letting Satan defeat me and rob me of my joy. Life had been hard, but I had something I did not have before. I had a living relationship with God, and he would pull me through. I simply had to put my trust in him.

As Harvey and I continued our involvement with the church, I felt God speak to me, telling me I'd become a missionary someday. The idea excited me. *God, are you calling me somewhere? Overseas, perhaps?* One day, our old pastors, Benito and Jennifer, texted me. They were getting ready to start a church in Round Rock, just outside Austin.

"So, are you going to Round Rock with us?" they asked.

I sucked in my breath. During my prayer time one day, I'd felt God tell me I'd once again work with Jennifer and Benito. Was it time now? Was this the mission field he had for me?

I turned to Harvey, who was sitting beside me as I read the text.

"Do you feel like this is where we're gonna go?" he asked.

"Yes," I replied confidently, tears flowing down my cheeks.

I loved our church, we owned a nice house and Harvey's landscape business was thriving. I had grown comfortable in my bubble of friends, and the idea of leaving felt scary and sad. But it also excited me.

Since inviting Jesus into my heart, I had learned to surrender my life and my plans to him. It didn't always mean taking the easy way out, but instead it involved believing that God would take care of me and trusting him, even when I could not see the road ahead.

After much prayer, Harvey and I decided to make the move to Round Rock. We packed our things, said goodbye to our beloved community and prepared for yet another adventure.

RESCUED

I was excited to see what God had for us in the growing town of Round Rock, my new mission field.

But more twists and turns awaited our arrival.

❧❧❧

Harvey and I settled into Round Rock, enjoying the family-friendly community just outside the bustling city of Austin. We struggled to find jobs upon our initial move. Harvey finally landed a job and took over as manager of a storage facility, and we lived in the apartment on the grounds. I volunteered in the office at our new church, Freedom Church, and enjoyed meeting new people.

It was exciting to be a part of something new. The pastors sensed my enthusiasm and trusted me with even more duties. I could not have been happier with my new role. Harvey began volunteering as an usher at the church and enjoyed his position as well. Though we'd dearly loved our church near Dallas, I was happy to find a new place to call home.

Just as we settled in, however, my health began to decline. The doctors diagnosed me with Graves' disease, a thyroid disorder. They prescribed medication, but as my condition worsened, they gave me two more drastic options.

"You need to take this radioactive iodine or undergo thyroid removal surgery."

I didn't want to do either. I continued to pray, asking God for wisdom. I knew I could not stay on my medication forever, as it produced very bad side effects. I'd have to make a decision sooner than later.

I met with the doctor again, and he suggested I get off my medication in preparation for taking the radioactive iodine. I did as he instructed. At a church staff meeting, I asked the pastors and leaders to pray for me. They asked God to heal me, and I believed he could. *A miracle would be great, God!*

Several weeks later, I went to get my blood drawn. Later that day, I went back to visit the doctor for my results. Just before I got out of my van, I stopped to pray. "God, you healed me of cancer, and I ask you to heal me right now. Whatever your desire is for me, I accept it."

A fourth-year medical student surveyed my blood work after I arrived. He scrunched his face, looking perplexed. "Are you still on your medication?" he asked.

I shook my head. "No, the doctor told me to stop taking it."

"Huh. I'll be right back." He went to get the doctor.

The doctor came in and studied the results. "Your labs are in the normal range. I don't understand. It looks like your condition is in remission."

My heart filled with joy at his words. He didn't understand, but I did. My God had healed me! My Graves' disease, considered treatable but incurable, had been miraculously reversed. *Thank you, God! You are so good!*

I called Harvey first, and then my stepfather, to deliver the good news. "I'm healed!" I cried, overjoyed. "God healed me without medication or surgery!"

RESCUED

Next, I called Pastor Benito. We rejoiced together, both certain in the belief that God was completely at work.

At Freedom Church, we like to say that we are a refuge for "jacked-up" people. I am one of those people. I came from brokenness, and my pain was once so great I wanted to die. I tried numbing that pain with drugs, booze and false love, but I always turned up empty and alone. And then I fell in love with Jesus. He healed my wounded heart and my broken relationships, even with my mother. He offered hope and joy in place of my sadness. In the darkness, I called out to him, begging him to relieve me from the hurt. But I now trust that he was there all along. He was just waiting for me to climb onto the rope so he could pull me up.

I have been rescued.

THE STATISTIC
The Story of Joseph
Written by Marty Minchin

"Kids, get upstairs!" My dad shooed us once again into a different part of the house.

What is going on here? I wondered as Jack, Missy and I traipsed out of sight and hearing of the four adults playing cards and drinking in the living room.

Mom and Dad had become instant best friends with, of all people, the man who drove the public bus route through our neighborhood and his wife. I'd seen the guy countless times when I got on and off the bus. He'd sometimes let us poor kids slip by without paying the fare, and I'd often ride the bus late at night to the end of the line and back just to get out of the neighborhood for a while.

"Something's going on," I confided in Jack as we sat down in the bus driver's bedroom. Why else would we be coming over to this house three nights in a row? We'd never socialized with this family before.

Jack nodded in agreement, and we mulled over the situation in silence.

We didn't have to wait long. The screaming, mostly from my tiny Italian mom, started in the kitchen. Then Dad was screaming, and we kids started screaming when we ran in to see what was going on.

Mom waved a gun around — the same gun the bus driver carried on the bus in case someone tried to rob the fare box. If she had a target, it didn't seem to be the bus driver's wife, who my dad apparently had just admitted to having an affair with.

"How could you?" Mom yelled at Dad, her high-pitched sounds rising over the clamor. "What were you thinking?"

Then Mom was running with the gun, out the door of the condo into the night.

"Mom, don't!" I took off after her, not sure if she was going to shoot me or shoot herself. When a gunshot rang out, I stopped in my tracks.

❧❧❧

As a teenager, my mom moved from Framingham, Massachusetts, to Portsmouth, Virginia, when her father was transferred there with the Navy. She was a tiny woman, only 4 feet, 10 inches, and her dark hair and petite figure caught my dad's eye in high school. They started dating when they were 16, likely unaware that their combined family histories already were shaping the future for the babies they soon would conceive.

Growing up in a military family, Mom was used to being around men who drank. Dad had grown up watching his parents get drunk and hash it out with each other physically. Their teenage union quickly produced me, and after deciding not to abort, they rushed into marriage and dropped out of high school. Missy was born two and a half years later, followed by two more brothers. We lived in a series of low-income houses in the poor and rundown corners in and around Suffolk, and each dwelling was filled with violence and surrounded by drugs, crime and sex. One bright spot was my grandmother, who would take us to church when we visited her and talk to us about religious things. As my world filled up with negativity, my grandmother remained a reminder that hope and optimism were possible.

My parents were ill-prepared to provide a stable home, and our exposure as kids to poverty, violence and neglect set us up for a future as high school dropouts and substance-abusing statistics. My brothers and sister and I were largely on our own. When we needed to do laundry, I would lead my caravan of siblings on a mile walk to the Laundromat. We each lugged a trash bag of dirty clothes, and we'd use our food stamps to buy gum and get change for the machines. The four of us would play while the washers and dryers ran, and then we'd fold our clothes and walk home. We tried to take care of the few items of clothing we did have, but our raggedy appearance left no question that we were poor kids. A big shopping day for us was when the shoe store sold Converse sneakers at two pair for $5.

By the time I was in third grade, I was a streetwise kid. I spent hours roaming the neighborhood and frequently stayed out until 1 or 2 a.m. When I did go home, I usually let myself in with my own key. I wasn't sure where my parents were half the time, and sometimes it was just easier to stay with friends. By third grade, I was smoking and using drugs, which was not a big deal because nearly every house I went into was inhabited by someone who drank, smoked and usually did drugs, too. When I got old enough to sell drugs, I did some dealing to help pay for my own habits.

The late 1960s brought integration to the South, but in the poor suburbs of Southeastern Virginia, my family was already unintentionally doing its part. I was one of few white kids in an African-American neighborhood, and I hung out with a diverse group of friends. At school, I didn't fit in with the wealthy white kids, who just needed to take one look at my threadbare clothes to know that I wasn't one of them. As I got older, I told people I was one of the "white brothers." I grew my hair out past my shoulders and combed it with a "rake," a wide-tooth plastic comb popular with my black friends.

My dad's side of the family did occasionally like to get together, and our gatherings followed the same pattern: drinking, fighting and cops. One of my uncles had fought in Vietnam, and he was never the same when he got home from the war. A couple of hours of drinking mixed with an unstable uncle usually led to drunken brawling. The calling of the cops was inevitable — family parties almost always ended with the blue lights rolling into the driveway.

My mom sometimes took us to her mother's house, but if the rest of her family had a party, we generally

THE STATISTIC

weren't invited. They were well-to-do and lived in nice homes, and we wore old clothes and lived in apartments and ghetto houses. The few times we did see our relatives, our jeans with holes and dirty shoes once again gave away our lower economic status.

When I did lift my head up long enough to look down the path ahead of me in life, it looked like it led only one way. I was an outcast wherever I went, and I had resigned myself to a journey that didn't lead any further than the next drug-infested block.

෨෨෨

"Hey, kid!" A young, clean-cut white guy had pulled up on our street in a white van.

I stopped my bike and hopped off.

"Are you going to come to church with us?" This guy didn't fit in here. He clearly was educated, and he was well-spoken and dressed nicely.

I'd been to church a few times with my grandmother, who also had put on TV shows about Jesus and Bible stories for us. It seemed like a good place.

"Sure, why not?" I told him.

"I'm Brother Mark," he said. "I'll be here at nine sharp tomorrow morning to pick some kids up."

My first trip to church with him turned into a regular outing. I liked going to church with Brother Mark. He'd drive through the neighborhood and pick kids up, although sometimes it was only me and my brothers and sister who showed up. We sang songs on the bus, and I felt like we were driving to a wonderland that was on the other side of the world from the hell we lived in on the streets. At church, no one yelled at us or put us in closets as punishment. We had snacks and hung out with groups of other children. We learned about the Bible and sometimes went to "big church" with the adults.

When Brother Mark came around to remind the kids he'd be by the next morning with the bus, I made sure I was ready. I took a bath the night before, carefully parting my thick, puffy hair on the side. I pulled out my best shirt — a spring-colored plaid button-down — and, of course, my two for $5 Converse tennis shoes.

One of those Sundays at the Baptist church, I felt like I truly connected with God for the first time. I had always believed that there was a God, and sometimes I talked to him. I talked to God that day, asking him to be in charge of my life.

I wanted everything God offered. I wanted to feel clean and go to heaven because I felt a lot of pain on earth. I wanted to live somewhere happy, and heaven seemed ideal.

When I stood up out of the water after the pastor baptized me, I saw the joy on the faces of the people in the church. I knew that God had forgiven me for smoking pot, hitting my brothers and sister, stealing from stores and everything else I had done wrong. As the water dripped down my face, I broke into a huge smile.

Unfortunately, no one in my family was there to see it.

THE STATISTIC

Outside of the church, my life continued to be difficult. Dad had an affair with the bus driver's wife, and even though I think Mom suspected it, she was shocked when Dad told her about it after a few nights of cards and drinks with his mistress and her husband.

"No!" I screamed as I heard the gun fire outside the bus driver's house. Who was her target?

She had shot into the air, and then the gun was quiet.

Mom was checked into a mental institution, and the bus driver's kids eventually became my stepbrothers.

After Mom was committed, I lived with an uncle for a few months and then shuffled between friends' houses. Mom came home, resettled in her house and started dating.

Even though they were separated and Dad was with the bus driver's wife, he didn't like the idea of her being with another man. Sometimes at night, we'd watch through the window as his car drove slowly by our house, my dad and his uncles peering inside to see if my mom had company.

The night my dad upped his game from stalker to attacker plays like a disjointed, flickering film in my mind.

Dad and his brothers bursting in the door.

Mom and her boyfriend, running naked through the house.

Glass raining onto the floors as the men busted out the windows.

Cowering in the corner under a blanket, praying for an escape route.

My tiny mom, unclothed, trying to fight off my dad.

The nauseating sight of the boyfriend's head being bashed into the toilet bowl.

And, as always, the blue lights of the police cars.

We were evicted from the house and left the neighborhood, but we moved into another den of drug dealers and delinquents. Dad and his new wife didn't live far away, but he still wouldn't leave my mom and us alone. When he was drunk, which was often, he'd come over and cause all sorts of trouble.

My only option, I decided, was a gamble. I moved in with Dad, figuring I could endure all of his drinking and violence, if it meant he'd stay away from Mom's house and the littler kids.

A year later, I found out that he'd been going over to Mom's, anyway, beating her up while my brothers and sister cried. Settling deeper into my seat on the train wreck of my life, I almost put my dad in the hospital before I moved out.

I was starting high school, but I rarely went. I moved from friend's couch to friend's couch, and when the couches weren't available, I lived in a car. If I had a girlfriend, I'd stay with her. I drank harder and did more drugs.

When I got my license, my friends and I hit as many concerts as we could. The large population of young men living at the Navy port near Norfolk could easily fill a stadium, and the country's biggest hip-hop and rock and roll bands came through town at least once a week.

Sometimes I talked to God. With my family all but disappearing, I longed to fill that hole inside me. Life, however, was a powerful magnet that easily pulled me away.

When I was 16, I went MIA from my family. It was almost too easy to steal money from my dad's house and hop a ride to Miami with a friend. We moved into a hotel, where the Cuban owner said we could live in exchange for doing some work for him. At the time, some people from Haiti regularly smuggled bales of marijuana into Miami, and the pot was plentiful. But when the money ran out eight months later, we hitchhiked back to Virginia where, for me, feelings of loneliness set back in.

I wasn't violent. I wasn't hurting anyone. But I wasn't doing any good. I had no direction, and I was basically killing myself abusing drugs and alcohol. So when my mom and my new stepdad issued a last-chance offer to me to move to Pennsylvania and live with them, I took it.

෯෯෯

I quickly got mixed up with the wrong kids in Pennsylvania, and before long, I got into trouble at school and ended up before a judge. I had just turned 18, and I was old enough to be tried as an adult. The judge gave me an ultimatum: Go to jail, or go into the military.

It was time to give myself another chance. The military

can be a cold place, and many people I met thought enlisting was a big mistake. For me, it was a godsend.

Joining the Army was like booking a one-man vacation for myself. The only military flare-up going on in the world at the time was unrest over the Falkland Islands, and I was stationed in the United States then. I traveled to California and Germany and had plenty of time on my own. Highly structured days replaced 18 years of constant moving and uncertainty, and for once, my mind began to settle down and clear.

I had no girlfriend, no family that I particularly wanted to see and at best a weak connection to God. But I wanted to get to know God better, and now I had enough focus to talk to him regularly through prayer. I asked God to show me a direction in my life and to forgive me for the wrong things I had done.

People think that the Army is like one big fraternity with guys everywhere to hang out with, but that's not necessarily true. If you don't get to know anyone, you're on your own, and I kept to myself. When I was stationed in Germany, I couldn't speak the language other than the little I'd learned in a two-week crash course. It was hard to make friends there, and I didn't try much.

When holidays rolled around and guys happily headed home, I stayed on base and went out to clubs or to see movies. Sometimes I just sat in my barracks, or if I wanted to get out, I would go for a long run. I was adrift, disconnected from other people while I tried to set my feet on the right path. Prayer became a rope that anchored me to God, and when I found myself feeling empty or disconnected, I started talking to God more and became more focused and secure in the choices I was making.

I also started to go to church while I was in the Army. Sometimes I went with two or three other guys, but I often went alone. Church helped me spend time with God, and I knew that as my life began to take a positive turn that God was a big part of it.

The day I got out of the Army, I felt more focused than I ever had. I had found my path, and it led toward God.

৯৯৯

While in the Army, I'd earned my GED, and I was ready to continue my education. I moved to a small town in Texas and enrolled in junior college. I rented a place with a couple of guys and still partied sometimes, but I knew now what following God felt like.

Even living in Texas couldn't get the hip-hop and rock and roll out of me, and when I found myself at a country-western joint one night, I knew I was out of place. My buddies drank, but as the designated driver, I stayed at the table with my glass of Coke.

When two Hispanic girls walked by my table, I looked up. I'd spent most of my life as the shy guy, but the Army had taught me that an important part of showing respect was making eye contact with other people. I mustered my courage and looked one of the girls in the eye and smiled. She smiled back.

Something felt different inside. I wanted to know her, maybe for a long time.

I stood up and followed the girls across the bar.

"Do you want to dance?" I asked the one who had smiled. I had never danced country-western in my life, but I was willing to start now for a chance to talk to her.

We strolled out onto the floor, and she helped me two-step. At the end of the evening, she gave me her phone number, which I promptly lost.

I spent days racking my brain for a memory of where I might have put that slip of paper. The memory — and the paper — were gone, but she had told me that she worked at Anthony's, a clothing store with several locations in the area.

It was worth a shot. Two weeks after we met, I ordered flowers and had them sent to an Anthony's, even though I didn't know if she worked there or if she'd accept the flowers.

As a kid, I had frequently given my mom and my sister and brothers flowers and pictures and other little gifts. I tried to have a good heart and love my family well.

"Woohoo, Lydia!" Her fellow employees shouted and clapped as I came into the store looking for her. Her shy smile was all I needed to know: I had found her, and she was glad to see me.

Lydia was 27, three years older than me, and she had a hard-scrabble background like me. She'd married young and had two sons, and her ex-husband had abandoned them soon after the youngest one was born.

THE STATISTIC

The more we got to know each other, the more we wanted to know. We went to movies, and I spent time with her boys, who seemed accepting of me as a potential father figure. I took two semesters of two-step classes at my college, and I even bought myself some real cowboy boots. I was in love.

We spent a lot of time with her big Hispanic family. Her dad wasn't sure about her bringing home a white guy, but now he loves me.

Lydia and I married and had a daughter and son. I raised her older sons as my own, coaching their soccer and baseball teams. I never adopted them or asked them to change their last name, but sometimes they wrote my last name as theirs, and sometimes people called me by their last name.

It didn't matter. We were family either way.

వొవొవొ

Lydia and I had our ups and downs in marriage, but we raised our children in a stable middle-class lifestyle and gave them options I never dreamed of as a kid. When our daughter was struggling to take care of her two babies on her own, we felt privileged to be able to take in the girls and raise them as our own. We watched our granddaughters grow up and talked about following through on our longtime hope of strengthening our relationships with God. We knew it was time to seek out God and other people who believed in him.

FREEDOM STORIES

Our first step was to get back to church. We knew a few people who attended Freedom Church, so we tried it out. Walking in the door, the sense of *rightness* overcame me, just like when I met Lydia.

The congregation reminded me of a better version of the world I grew up in. The faces there were as diverse as those of my childhood neighbors. I could wear old, torn-up clothes if I wanted, and no one would care. The church was welcoming and full of acceptance, like a family that loved you no matter what you looked like or who you were.

We've joined a small discussion and prayer group, and I serve as an usher at Freedom Church. The young adults at the church are the same age as my children, and I like how they talk to me and listen to what I have to say. I watch them help each other stay focused on living their lives God's way so that they don't get off track or lost in the shuffle.

When I watch these young people, I often wish I had brought my children to church when they were growing up. I'm thankful that my grandmother and, in her own way, my mom tried to exert a positive influence on me, despite the difficult circumstances around them, and I'm glad I still have the opportunity to help my children choose a good path.

The closer I've gotten to Jesus, through reading the Bible and talking to him, the more connected I feel to God and to other people. I know that I was a statistic. Now, I'm a child of God.

THE STATISTIC

When Lydia and I walk into church holding the hands of our young grandchildren, it feels awesome. They are like little treasures — the beautiful, tangible evidence of God's amazing work in my life.

THE MAN
The Story of Dave Maniaci
Written by Arlene Showalter

"I am Dave Maniaci." I lay on my bed, rested my head on my hands and stared up at the ceiling. The events of the past few hours flooded back, and I savored each moment like a perfectly grilled steak.

Tournament game. I shot at 100 percent, zipping up and down the court like a hungry cougar. Nobody, but nobody could match my shooting and dribbling skills. I had jumped and released the ball a nanosecond before the final buzzer.

Swish. Two points and game! Our home-team crowd erupted from the bleachers with an appreciative roar and hoisted me high in the air on tall shoulders.

I grinned. I had arrived at the ripe age of 12.

"I am *the man!*"

☙☙☙

"Swing, Daddy, swing," I chanted when Dad took the plate for his local softball league. I studied his movements. *Tap the bat against the foot. Tap it against the plate.* My 5-year-old hands curled around an imaginary bat as Dad lifted his behind his head. "Swing, Daddy, swing."

My first sports opportunity arrived in first grade. Although small for my age, I was quicker than the bigger guys and far more aggressive. I immediately excelled at football, basketball and baseball as I advanced through elementary school. By sixth grade, I was elected team captain of the three sports, and it stayed that way through high school graduation.

Athletic prowess, popularity and girls. I possessed it all and knew it. My accomplishments and ego kept pace like Stockton and Malone.

In my junior year, I had the ball firmly under my capable hand in a fast dribble. My opponent matched my pounding steps as I charged toward the basket. We slammed into each other, and he fell on his back. I stood over him, dribbling and grinning.

"Get up! Let's try that play again."

He stared up at me. I turned toward Coach and yelled, while maintaining my dribble. "I'm gonna beat this guy."

Coach scowled. My grin widened. *He'll be lecturing me again about my attitude.* My eyes swept the stands, crammed with eager fans. I shrugged. *They're all here to see me play, so he'll just have to deal with it.*

"That was some game," I said to my parents on the drive home. "You see how I juked the ball and faked that guy out?"

"Dave," Mom said. "You need to be careful. God gave you the ability to play sports. You should recognize that and thank him for it."

Yeah, right. I gazed out the window. *I put that game in the bag for the team. Me. Dave Maniaci.*

THE MAN

❧❧❧

The recruiters started buzzing around our games in 10th grade.

"Come to our college," each begged me. "We have the best sports program in the state."

I'm Dave Maniaci. I'm the man, dude. I don't need you. You need me. I'll go wherever I choose and play whatever sport I want.

But love won out, and I chose the University of Toledo, which hadn't offered me a sports scholarship, to live close to home and Laura, my girlfriend.

I'll get a degree in communications and become a play-by-play announcer. Like sliding into second base. The networks will be all over me, just like the recruiters were. I'll have my pick of jobs.

Six months later, Laura called. "We're through."

"What?" *You're breaking up with me? Dave Maniaci?*

"There's nothing to discuss. It's over."

"Well, what about that scrapbook you made of newspaper clippings? Can I at least have that back?"

"Too late. I threw it out."

No girlfriend. No sports. I jumped into the frat scene with the enthusiasm of running the winning touchdown and earned a reputation for partying hard. My ego matched my movements, step by step.

"Watch out, you moron," I snapped at an underclassman who bumped me in the hall.

"Sorry, dude." He slunk away.

Some friends and I were walking across campus when a kid on crutches fell in front of us. I kept walking.

"Hey, dude," one of my friends said. "You feeling bad?"

"Why do you ask that?"

"No comments on the klutz?"

"Huh?"

"You losing your touch? You never bypass the opportunity to smack a person down."

"Hey, everybody, this is Dave Maniaci from Toledo Rocket Country. Stay tuned for complete coverage of tonight's game."

To stay close to the sports scene, I began hosting a show on campus that covered the Toledo Rockets, the university's basketball team. I covered every game by interviewing the coach and key players. Then I went on the air with the hour-long show.

After four years, I clutched my highly prized degree in my hand. *Now the sports executives will be begging me to join their broadcasting team, just like the recruiters did in high school. Everybody wants Dave Maniaci on his team. Life is good.*

I knocked on doors. Lots of doors. All remained closed to *me*, Dave, *the man.*

A friend offered me a job working construction. *What's going on here?* I leaned on my shovel, standing in another endless ditch. *I was made for better stuff than this.*

THE MAN

Then I relaxed. *I can make this happen. I'll get that dream job. I know who I am.*

࿇ ࿇ ࿇

"Dave, we are going to the Gugliottas' this Saturday," Mom said soon after I finished college. "They're having a graduation party for Michelle."

The Gugliotta and Maniaci families were close friends. We attended the same church, and we always attended each other's functions, parties and celebrations.

"I've already endured two of their kids' high school graduations," I groaned. "I'm 23. I shouldn't have to go."

Mom studied my face. "They're our good friends. You're going."

I took my attitude to the party — until I came face to face with Michelle. *Holy cow. When did you grow up?* I studied her throughout the party.

"You think you'd ever want to go out with me?" I asked her as my family prepared to leave.

Michelle knew all about Dave Maniaci. Her father, Tony, had followed my sports career, both on the sidelines and in the paper. He sat in the stands with my parents at many games. However, my popularity left his daughter unimpressed.

Michelle also knew about my string of girlfriends. Even though she showed no interest in me for many months, I still pursued her. Eventually, she agreed to a double date with another couple.

Because of the construction job, I could afford to take Michelle to Cleveland Indian baseball games and nicer restaurants than what she was accustomed to.

I pursued Michelle with the same intensity I'd poured into sports and soon determined to make her my wife. After 18 months of dating, I contacted the marketing director (whom I knew) of the Cleveland Cavaliers with a plan.

I talked Michelle into going to a Cavaliers basketball game and coaxed her to sit in the exact seat the director had assigned. I had bought the entire first row and filled it with friends.

"Why do I have to sit here? I want to sit with the girls at the other end."

"Just sit here through the first quarter," I coaxed. "You can do that for me, can't you?"

"Why do I have to sit on this end seat?"

"Just for now. Please."

"Okay." She flopped down and crossed her arms.

The first quarter ended. Suddenly a cartoon character flashed on the screen with a bow and arrow. He shot at a heart, which burst into the words, "I love you."

All the house lights dimmed until a single spotlight shone on Michelle and me. I pulled a ring from my sock and knelt in front of her while 13,000 fans looked on.

"Will you marry me?" Nerves played a frightened tune in my belly. *What if she refuses in front of all these people?*

She put my mind and stomach at ease.

THE MAN

"Yes."

The whole arena erupted in applause and whistles. Every player from both teams came over to congratulate us.

We married a year later, in 1986.

☙☙☙

"I have some marketing expertise," I told my uncle, Mike, who owned and operated Migelitos Pizza on a prime corner in Cleveland. "How about if I work for you and help build up your business?"

"That sounds like a good plan." I became his manager and helped build the business from 20 employees to 80. My competitiveness in sports helped give me the insight to grow the business, enabling me to double it in my first year there. I started a catering truck division that grew from one vehicle to five in that time, and the business exploded.

We sold a good product at a decent price because Uncle Mike owned the lot on which the pizza shop stood, thus avoiding the expense of rent.

"Come on, Dave, let's pray together before we open for the day." Uncle Mike loved and honored God like my parents did.

"Okay." As soon as he turned to go into his office, I rolled my eyes. *Let's get this daily routine over with so I can get on with work.*

I found putting up with Uncle Mike's prayer to begin

the daily routine annoying, yet doable. However, he never left his "religion" in the office, but carried it into the dining room where he circulated and chatted with his customers.

"Hey, Dave, come out here, and help me pray for this customer," became as common as pepperoni on pizza.

This sucks. What if somebody I know sees me? My reputation will be down the toilet.

I'd drag myself to where Uncle Mike stood and "helped" him pray for the customer in need. We prayed for people facing surgery, bad backs, broken bones and fractured hearts.

ক্তক্তক্ত

Uncle Mike had a superior product and superb location. Money flowed into the shop as pizzas rolled out. I enjoyed a stable income, and Michelle gave birth to our first son, Andrew, three years after our marriage.

I maintained the façade of living like I thought a Christian should, but I put my friends, sports and other interests first.

Michelle took the position of spiritual leader in the home, truly honoring God with her life.

"You're digging a hole, Dave," she warned many times. "You do not give God glory for your accomplishments. He can't bless our family until you get your act together."

ক্তক্তক্ত

THE MAN

"Saturday's our last day." Uncle Mike approached me on a Monday, five years after I'd started working for him. "I sold the shop."

"What?" I stared at him blankly. "What do you mean Saturday's our last day? You're making a killing here." *How am I supposed to support my family?*

"Sorry, Dave, but Lube Stop wants this corner and made me an offer I couldn't refuse."

"How much?"

"One point two million. Cash."

"You're kidding."

"No. That's a lot of money. Plenty for me to find another place to open up a pizza shop."

My uncle sold.

Lube Stop knocked the building down a week later.

Uncle Mike searched for a new place, but his love for cars prompted him to begin a whole new sort of business other than a restaurant.

"I'm going to open a yogurt place," I informed Michelle. "We'll be in on the ground floor because the craze is just taking off."

"You make all your decisions without praying first," she said. "God wants you to come to him and seek his counsel."

And your point is? I kept my comments to myself and forged ahead with Dave's plans by taking our savings and opening up two yogurt shops. We made a huge profit our first year.

"Didn't I tell you I'd take care of you and make things happen? I'm making better money than I did with Uncle Mike."

The following year, I *lost* $64,000. And Michelle gave birth to our second son, Austin.

"Now what will we do?" Michelle asked. "You should be asking God for direction rather than doing it all on your own."

"We'll be fine. I'll cut my losses and find another job." That took longer than I'd expected, and our bills piled up with no income to pay them all, forcing us to juggle them and begin relying on credit cards. Stress and anxiety dogged our family.

Michelle begged me to turn to God for guidance.

"You need to honor God first, through tithing," she insisted.

"How can giving God 10 percent of any money coming in help," I asked, "when our bills are so overwhelming?" I chose not to tithe.

In my desperate need for a job, I took a sales position in Orlando, Florida, which took us away from our family and friends. I promised Michelle the move would be temporary.

We moved to Orlando, but our hearts remained at home in Ohio. Michelle dragged the boys and me to a church that she had found. After hearing another message on tithing, I felt a nudge from God to obey, but still refused because my financial ends refused to meet.

The situation worsened. I unexpectedly lost my job.

THE MAN

Invincible Dave Maniaci had to file for unemployment, which didn't cover all our expenses. Debt double-dribbled over me, and I once again lost control of the ball of success.

I walked through the kitchen of our rental and spotted an empty box in the trash can.

"What's this?" I demanded.

"I bought a Happy Meal for Andrew. It was only $1.99."

"$1.99?" I roared. "Are you kidding me?"

"This isn't what I signed up for when I married you." Anger and tears shone in Michelle's eyes. "We weren't raised this way, and you know it. We were raised to honor God and seek his guidance."

"I can't pay the rent," I told our landlord. "I've searched all over for a job but haven't found one yet."

"Your problem." He shrugged. "You signed the lease, so you're still on the hook."

Michelle spent countless hours on the phone, complaining to her mother. I forged ahead on "Dave's brilliance and steam."

After applying for work all over Florida, I branched out to other states. Motorola in Austin, Texas, contacted me and flew me in for an interview.

"You realize what a long shot this is?" I asked Michelle. "You know Motorola is interviewing internal candidates first."

"Then I'm going to pray that if it's God's will for you to get the job, you will."

She did. I got the job. We relocated to Austin, Texas, and I started working three 12-hour shifts, Friday through Sunday. The move and job were brutal. We knew nobody in Austin. Soon Michelle started searching for a church, finally settling on one. She and the boys loved it there, but my work hours prohibited my going.

Six months after our move, Motorola experienced a massive layoff that included the once-invincible Dave Maniaci. Our failed-yogurt-shop debt had followed us to Texas and now hung over our heads like a menacing cloud.

It climbed to $60,000. I started jockeying credit cards once again, using the offered cash advance of one to pay the balance of another. I couldn't juke this opponent.

I've got to find a way to stop this financial bleeding. I took us from our families. Michelle cries to her mother all the time over the phone. I feel like we're living on an ever-shrinking island where the tide of debt continues to rise and never goes back out.

"Dave, I've watched you all these years." Michelle took a chair across the table from me as I stewed over the bills. Desperation shimmered in her dark eyes. "You've played at being a Christian all these years, but you don't truly rely on God. You rely on Dave Maniaci. Are you even a Christian?"

"Of course," I snapped.

THE MAN

"What does 'being a Christian' mean to you, then?"

My mind went back to when I was 11. A guest preacher came to our home church. "Exodus 20:12 reads, 'Honor your father and mother so that your days may be long upon the land ...'"

Ouch. Even at that age, my ego increased with every basket, touchdown and home run and manifested with cocky words and attitude. *Busted.*

"If you feel God speaking to you tonight, please raise your hand," the preacher continued.

I obeyed. Two lone hands joined mine. I wanted to melt into the pew.

"Those who raised their hands, please come forward. We want to pray with you."

What do I do now? I'm Dave Maniaci. I can't announce my imperfections to the world. However, my legs straightened to stand, and my feet carried me to the front.

The speaker prayed with me, while my parents expressed keen delight over me making a public commitment to Christ.

But I pretty much left God at the altar, only praying in earnest when I needed something from him — which was seldom — since I had a good grip on where I expected to take myself in life.

Mom and Dad had tried to reel in my ego as I continued to excel in all sports.

Press coverage increased, and the stands filled with people eager to see me play.

"You should give God the glory," Mom would say. "He gave you your amazing ability."

Once, when my team was in the biggest game of the year — the playoffs — I made three baskets in the first few minutes of the game. Then as I pounded down the court for my next shot, my ankle twisted. *For no reason.* I hobbled to the sidelines and watched our team, *my* team, lose.

"God's trying to get your attention," Mom had said on the ride home.

Could it be? I frowned at nothing, but then shook my head. *Nah. It was just a fluke.*

Years later, Michelle's soft words slammed into my bruised ego.

"You're right," I finally admitted. "It can't get any worse. What should I do?"

"You need to get your heart clean before God," she said. "Recommit your life to him. Every situation needs to be brought to God before you make a decision."

"Okay," I said.

"You've taken all your blessings for granted. Your talent. Your success." One lone tear trembled on her full, dark lashes, lost its grip and tumbled down her cheek. "This isn't what I signed up for. I don't deserve this. The boys don't deserve this. We have too much at stake to let you mess it up any further."

"You are absolutely right. I promise you now that I am releasing all power and control of my life — our lives — to God at this very moment."

THE MAN

"You need to honor that commitment with tithing," she continued.

"Tithing? Like give up 10 percent of our money to God?" My eyebrows stretched north. "With all this debt?"

"Yes. You need to prove you are serious with God by trusting him with our money first."

"First. As in before we pay a single bill?"

"Yes."

The next unemployment check arrived. I held it in one hand and our bundle of bills in the other. "God," I prayed. "I'm broke. Not just broke as in I have no money, but broke as in a broken man. I need a miracle. Besides our fixed bills, I'm in major debt. I'll never get out of this." My eyes searched the ceiling. "Lord, if you can make this happen, make it happen."

This time, rather than jumping at the first job opportunity, Michelle and I asked our pastor to pray with us. "I can't afford to do what I've done in the past," I said. "I have to trust God to provide and to help us survive the mess we're in."

Unemployment ran out. We continued hemorrhaging money. My wife, along with some men in our church, continued to pray over every potential job opportunity.

Cripe! How long can this go on?

Finally, a job offer came from Dallas, two hours away.

"Honey," I said, "I have to take this. For my manhood. I have to provide for my family. I have to get rid of our debt."

She agreed. Her sister had moved into that area, so I

stayed with them to save money. Then the company offered us a relocation package. This time I stopped to pray over it, but neither Michelle nor I felt any peace in our hearts about moving to Dallas. So while working there and commuting home on my days off, I began applying for jobs back in Austin. Seven months later, Solectron hired me as a supervisor, and I returned to Austin.

ॐॐॐ

Debt, though we paid off what we could, still harassed me. Faithfully, with every paycheck, I wrote out a tithe check.

God, we really need this money. We could pay off the debt so much faster if we didn't have to tithe. Bitterness and anger gnawed at me. *Can't I just miss this one time and make it up later?*

Michelle saw my scowl. "We have to honor God first."

Two years later, another company called me, asking if I would take a position as manufacturing manager and oversee 600 employees. The new job increased my income by $20,000 a year. *Thank you, Lord. That will help ease the debt.*

"We've got to find a way to stop the credit bloodbath," I said to Michelle one night in our family room. "Even though the new job helps, we aren't paying it back fast enough. Holy cow, it would be so nice to have it off our back."

"God will honor you for honoring him through tithing."

"You know, there are so many electronic components just lying around warehouses," I said. "Wouldn't it be great to find a way to buy and resell them?"

I jumped up. "I'm going to call one of my customers and ask him."

The customer confirmed my thought. "We have tons of parts sitting around," he said, "and I know for a fact we're never going to use them. We'd be happy to sell them to you."

"Can you send me a list?" I asked.

"Sure thing."

I showed it to my super-techie friend, Paul. "Can you look this over for me? Do you think there's opportunity to make a profit here?"

"Absolutely."

Paul checked off the viable products, and I went back to the customer. "How much do we need to purchase these?"

"Six grand."

I called Paul. "Guy wants six grand. You want to go in on this with me?"

"You bet."

I financed my $3,000 with a credit card, believing deep in my heart that if God had given me this idea, he would come through to address my financial situation. Not Dave Maniaci's brilliance this time, but God's.

We liquidated *all* of our debt with one transaction and

had money — a lot of money — left over. I showed the numbers to Michelle.

"God honors those who honor him." Her smile held more value to me than when I made that winning basket all those years before.

Six months after God helped us pay off our debt, Michelle and I decided to look for a house. We drove into a beautiful new subdivision.

"We could never afford any of this," I remarked.

"It costs nothing to look at the models."

"That's true."

Three contractors were building in the subdivision. We walked through the models that two of them offered. I noted the longing in Michelle's eyes and steeled myself against the inevitable truth.

After seeing what the first two contractors had to offer, we entered the site trailer of the third. Without a built model, the sales representative could only show us blueprints. Two house plans sat on a projected cul-de-sac.

"That would be so nice," Michelle said, as I studied the plans.

"One of these houses is $40,000 less than the other. Is there a typo here?"

"No, that's the price. And if you sign papers today, we'll waive the $10,000 fee for its location on the cul-de-sac."

I leaned forward to study the plans again.

"This is the largest lot in this area," I said, tapping the

blueprints with my finger. "How can it be so much cheaper?"

"It is," he insisted.

"What do you think?" I asked Michelle.

"I feel totally at peace about it. Let's do it."

"I agree."

We put down earnest money and returned home.

"I'm telling you, they goofed on that price."

"We've been praying for a house," Michelle said. "God knows the desires of our hearts. He owns the cattle on a thousand hills, and if he wants us to have this, he will make a way. It's no coincidence that you found a price discrepancy. I think God wants us to have this house."

Just trust me. I felt God speak into my heart. *I've got you covered. I brought this house to you.*

The contractor called us four weeks after we'd signed to purchase the house.

"You were right, Mr. Maniaci. The figure *was* a typo on the plans. But since you questioned it three times, the company has decided to honor your offer and give you the house at the original stipulated price."

"Who but God could give us a house with an instant $40,000 in equity?" I said to Michelle. "The Bible is right. 'As for God, his way is perfect'" (Psalm 18:30).

෧෧෧෧

I lost my father to cancer in 2006. When I was young and thought I was a hotshot, I neither cared for, nor understood Dad's integrity. Dad never made much money, yet he and Mom always invested time and money in their children before buying nice things for themselves.

When I floundered in debt after the yogurt shop failure, Dad took out a second mortgage on his home to pay off some of our credit cards and save us from finance charges.

When Michelle and I moved to Texas, Dad provided the down payment for a house. As the Lord humbled me through the financial disasters, I began to understand what a truly great man Dad was.

❧ ❧ ❧

We happily called the church in Austin "home" for 20 years. But after our move to Round Rock, the drive became too cumbersome.

"You've got to find a church closer to home," I said to Michelle. "With my hectic schedule, it just isn't feasible to drive so far. We pass a lot of churches on our way there. Surely we can find one closer to home so I can participate."

"You're right," she agreed. Soon, we had located Freedom Church, four miles from home. We respect Pastor Benito. We love the energy of a young and growing church. At 50-plus years, Michelle and I are the "old-timers."

"We bring age and maturity to this youthful congregation," I joke to Michelle.

THE MAN

I am hoping to live out my father's example, mentoring and helping when and where I can. Our own fiscal fiasco has left Michelle and me especially sensitive to people who are struggling in the same way, and we seek ways to help them. Our first question to each is, "Are you tithing?" Then we share the story of our experience with tithing.

God blessed me when I honored him, and I am now honored to bless others.

He's been faithful to his promise.

❧❧❧

"How about coming to church with us?" I asked a neighbor who had been going through a tough time in his marriage.

"Nah," he said, waving a dismissive hand. "Maybe some other time."

"This isn't about religion, it's about relationship. I used to be such an arrogant person, a know-it-all with a big head. Man, I thought I was untouchable. I thought I could do things without God."

I told him about some of my tough times and how God pursued me, even when I did not pursue him. I understood the pain and confusion when things go wrong.

"God had to pull the rug out from under me, my friend. It wasn't until I was completely broken that I cried out to him. He said, 'Here's my hand. Grab hold. It's always been there for you.' But I was so hard-headed, I wouldn't grab that hand until every one of my plans and schemes disintegrated."

I kept talking to him and praying. Our church hosted an outreach where we gave away $5 gift cards to Starbucks, along with an invitation to come to Freedom Church. I snuck an invitation in my neighbor's mailbox.

He showed up at Freedom Church.

"Man, it's so good to see you!"

"I figured that $5 Starbucks card came from you and Michelle."

After Pastor Benito's message, my friend's heart was touched, and God spoke a personal message to him for the struggles he was going through. I gave him a big hug and told him to give it to Jesus. His eyes welled up with tears because God changed his life that day.

"There was a time I thought I was *the man*," I told him. "That's before God got his hooks in me. I'm not the man. His name is Jesus, and *he's* The Man."

NO GOING BACK
The Story of Sunita
Written by Joy Steiner Moore

The loud ringing of the telephone shook me abruptly out of my sleep. I moaned and put my hands to my forehead, willing the migraine to go away. But when the phone rang again, the throbbing in my head only worsened.

Reluctantly, I reached over to my nightstand to answer it. I hated being disturbed after working a long night shift at the hospital, especially when I had a headache.

"Hello?"

"Hi, Sunita? This is Mrs. Williams from Natasha's school."

"Hello," I answered, trying to sound more awake than I felt.

"I'm so sorry, but we need you to come down to the school right away. Your daughter has, um ..." she paused, as if she was trying to come up with the right words, "suicidal ideas."

A gasp escaped my lips, and I felt a pang in my chest.

"Oh, my God! I will be right there!"

I stumbled out of bed and dressed as quickly as I could, in spite of my pounding head and the tears that blurred my vision.

Oh, Natasha!

The entire drive to the middle school, my heart broke

for my 12-year-old daughter, and I felt completely overwhelmed with grief and guilt for the way our lives had gone since moving to the United States. Between the culture shock and our struggling finances, our family was falling apart at the seams. My husband, Raj, and I were completely unhappy in our relationship, and our daughters were suffering.

How did I not see this coming?

I rushed into the school building and rounded the corner into the main office. There, sitting in a chair, was my precious girl, her silky black hair framing her lovely dark complexion. But as she looked up at me, the sadness and despair in her eyes made my heart ache. I gathered her into my arms.

"Oh, Mom!" she sobbed. "I'm so sorry."

"It's okay," I whispered. "It's going to be okay."

But in my heart, I didn't really know if it would be.

২৯২৯২৯

I was raised in a small village in Southern India. My family was very, very poor, though I didn't really understand how poor until I was much older.

We lived in a tiny house with mud walls and a dirt floor, where the seven of us siblings spread out blankets to sleep at night. We didn't have electricity until I was a teenager.

My father's job possibilities were limited due to his fourth grade education, so we didn't have enough food, and we frequently skipped meals. The feeling of hunger gnawing away at my stomach was a familiar one, but it didn't bother me too much — only because I didn't know anything different.

When I was 5 or 6, I began to understand that it wasn't normal to go without food. One day I went outside to play in front of my cousins' house, and my uncle called me over to where he sat.

"Sunita, did you eat breakfast today?"

I couldn't bring myself to meet his caring eyes. I was embarrassed but thought he must never know the truth.

"Yes," I lied, staring at the ground.

My uncle was quiet for a second, and I wondered what he was thinking.

"Okay. You may go play," he finally said, smiling kindly. But I felt so much shame.

৯৯৯

My father became an alcoholic, and any money he did earn was quickly lost on alcohol or gambling. Yet he believed in the importance of an education, and he required each of his children to finish school. He and my mom desperately wanted us to have a different and better life than they had, and they knew that education was the key.

Despite my difficult home life, I did well in my studies and was always at the top of my class. But when I finished 10th grade, my parents weren't sure they could afford the required monthly fee for me to go on to 11th and 12th grades. "You need to send her to school," my uncle told my father. "If you can't do it, I will pay for it myself."

And he did. For two years, my uncle paid 20 rupees a month, which was the equivalent of 40 cents, just so I could finish high school.

By this time, my oldest sister was living on her own and sending my family money, which she intended for our college education. She encouraged me to study nursing, so I applied to a program at a college our neighbor was attending. I was thrilled when I was accepted. The school was a day's journey from our village, but I liked the idea that I would know someone there.

College was a new experience for me in many ways. I was moving to a much larger city with many more modern conveniences than my village had. It was also a Christian college, and I was a Hindu. My father had always taught us that there was one God, but people worshiped him in different ways and with different names. He said that we should respect all religions, but it was his wish that we remain Hindus.

Out of 45 classmates, only three of us were Hindus. A new friend of mine was constantly trying to get me to convert to Christianity.

"I like Jesus," I told her. "But I'm not going to become a Christian."

"Yes, you will," she countered. "You'll become a Christian before you're done with your four years here."

I was very stubborn, and I took that as a challenge.

NO GOING BACK

಑಑಑

I graduated with my nursing degree, and true to my word, I had not become a Christian. But I wasn't really a Hindu anymore, either. I didn't believe in anything but science.

I got a job as a nurse first in India, then moved abroad to Muscat, Oman, in the Middle East, sending money home to help my younger brother and sister get an education, as my older sister had done for me. I also earned gold to put toward my dowry so I could hopefully get married someday. But things were getting worse at home. My father's alcoholism had gotten out of hand, and he would frequently abuse my mother and my sister. In addition, the money I sent for my dowry seemed to disappear. It was obvious that he was spending it on other things. I hated him for all of it.

When I was 30, my family finally arranged my marriage to Raj. I met him in my parents' house just nine days before our wedding day. He was a year and a half older than me, and he was from the same area of India. But unfortunately, it was not love at first sight. He struggled with depression, and he was very controlling. We didn't get along at all.

I returned to Muscat for my work, and Raj joined me. I hoped things would get better between us, but they didn't. He didn't have a job, which put a lot of pressure on me to be the breadwinner, a stress that was magnified after I gave birth to our daughter Natasha. Raj stayed home with the baby, but he was unhappy and angry all the time. Even after he did get a job, he was very difficult to live with.

Our home life was so depressing that I knew I didn't want to have any more children. It didn't make sense to add strain to a household filled with tension. I felt like I had to walk on tiptoes so as not to disturb Raj any more than Natasha's and my existence already did. The atmosphere in our home felt like a rubber band stretched to its capacity, ready to snap.

Nevertheless, when Natasha was 3 years old, I discovered I was pregnant again. Jasmine's birth brought a small measure of light and joy that I desperately needed.

In 2002, the threat of war in the Middle East made it a very difficult place to live. There were rumors that jobs would be cut, and with no savings, we knew we needed to get out while we still could. I didn't want to move back to India. Many of my friends were moving to the United Kingdom, Australia or the United States. There were a lot of nursing jobs available in the States, so we started the long application process. I believed that moving to the United States would be worth it in the long-run. Our daughters were guaranteed to have a better life there.

෬෬෬

After two years of paperwork, we were finally able to move to Round Rock, Texas, a community not far from Austin. We were glad to be out of the Middle East, but life was certainly not any greener on the other side of the proverbial fence. The same dark cloud hung over our family as before.

The nursing profession seemed different in America. I worked longer hours than I had in India or Muscat, and I worked night shifts, meaning that I had to sleep during the day. Between trying to ensure my family's smooth transition, adapting to a new job and getting very little sleep, I was stressed out all the time. I was overwhelmed by culture shock; everything was done differently than I was used to. The stress made me physically ill — my blood sugar was high, I suffered from migraines and I was constantly throwing up.

Raj wasn't able to work for the first couple of years, partially because we only had one car and he drove me to and from the hospital, and also because the girls were still young and needed a caregiver. This made him miserable and depressed. We fought often, and he became verbally abusive.

"Oh, because you have a job, you think you can talk to me like that?" was his response to almost anything I said.

I pictured our family as a sloppy-looking tapestry, poorly sewn together in the first place, and finally unraveling thread by thread.

꙼꙼꙼

We had only lived in the United States for about two or three years when the darkness started taking over

Natasha. She had always been a rather unhappy child, but this was different … more intense.

Testing done at the school concluded that she was suffering from depression and required counseling. But Raj didn't believe in therapy of any kind.

"She just needs a good beating," he said, anger in his voice. He often said mean things to Natasha, and responses like this made me think that maybe I should take the girls and move away from him. Maybe she just needed to be free from his constant badgering.

But against my better judgment, I stayed.

ৡৡৡ

It had been a long night shift, and I was exhausted. I collapsed on my bed and crawled under the covers, looking forward to the relief that sleep would bring my pounding head and nausea. But the phone call from the school changed everything.

Suicidal ideas? What does that mean? She's only 12!

I knew Natasha was depressed, but I had no idea it was *this* serious.

When I arrived at the school, I held my daughter for a few moments, wishing with all my heart that I knew how to take away the darkness that plagued her.

"Sunita, may I speak with you for a moment?" the school psychologist asked, nodding toward her office.

"Yes. Natasha, sweetheart, I will be right back," I said, gently guiding her back to a chair.

Mrs. Williams ushered me into a small office and closed the door behind her.

"Please have a seat," she offered kindly.

I sat down and folded my hands in my lap. I shifted uncomfortably in my seat. Even though I was Natasha's mother — the one who should be able to provide comfort to her child — I felt absolutely useless and helpless in this situation. This was unknown territory.

"Your daughter told me that she wants to kill herself but that she doesn't know how to do it," Mrs. Williams began. She sighed and shook her head. "She mentioned drinking a chemical in the bathroom, running away from home … she needs medical help as soon as possible. I would recommend taking her to the emergency room, and they can refer you to a mental hospital."

The room seemed to be spinning around me. Mrs. Williams' words echoed in my brain.

Drinking a chemical in the bathroom? Obviously, she can't be left alone!

"I agree," I finally managed. "I will take her there right now."

కకకక

Raj was at work, so I called him on our way to the hospital.

"You need to meet me at the ER right away," I told him, after filling him in.

"Okay, I will come later," he said, clearly unaffected.

He doesn't understand how serious this is! He makes me so angry! I fumed.

I turned my attention back to Natasha. Mrs. Williams had told me some of what was said, but I wanted to hear it for myself. Keeping my eyes on the road, I reached over and squeezed my daughter's hand.

"What's wrong, darling? What kinds of things are you thinking?" I asked gently.

"Well …" she paused. She looked down at her lap. "I get this thought in my head. It says, 'Go die.' But … I don't know how."

A chill crept up my spine, and my eyes widened.

Oh, my God.

Being a nurse, I was trained to believe that science and medicine could solve anything. But now, for the first time, I wasn't so sure. I felt like this was something beyond what science could help.

I wished for a moment that I believed in God. How nice would it be to believe that something big and powerful was on my side? Something bigger than science, something bigger than this darkness?

Raj met us at the local emergency room before we were sent 30 miles away to a mental hospital. I left our younger daughter, Jasmine, with a neighbor for the night, being incredibly vague as to the reason why. I didn't want anybody to know the ugly truth of the situation.

Raj and I drove to the mental hospital, and we got Natasha checked in. One of the hardest things we've ever had to do was leave our daughter there that night, but the staff assured us it was for the best. We checked into a nearby hotel and cried all night long.

"I never realized she was this ill!" Raj sobbed, finally understanding the severity of the situation.

No kidding.

I felt guilty for the chaos at home; it had definitely contributed to the problem. I wished I knew what to do to make our family peaceful and happy. There didn't seem to be an easy answer. In my mind, I blamed Raj for a lot of it.

Maybe we should separate, I thought. *His words can be so hurtful.*

The next five days were the longest and hardest of my life. I spent hours at Natasha's bedside, holding her hand, consulting with her doctors. The concern I felt for her was overwhelming. I wished I could physically lift the dark cloud that hung over her. But I was helpless.

In the midst of it all, I felt extremely alone. I couldn't tell any of our friends what was going on. I didn't want a rumor to get around that our daughter was mentally ill. If it did, her future could be jeopardized.

Raj and I managed to keep the situation between us, but since our relationship was practically non-existent, we couldn't even support each other. Again, I wished for something or someone to lean on. I wished that the caring God I had learned about back in college had truly existed.

But that's silly, I thought to myself. *He doesn't exist. You're on your own.*

❧❧❧

Natasha was sent home with several types of medication to assist with depression, but she still struggled for the next few years. She hated taking the medicine. We worked with the doctors to try different brands that might work better than others, but we could never find the right one, and her mood continued to be up and down.

"When I turn 18, I'm not going to take the pills anymore," she told me, her dark eyes defiant.

"Okay," I answered. "But you have to take them until you're 18, as long as you live in this house."

In the meantime, she saw a counselor. I also convinced Raj to start marriage counseling with me, but when he felt like the female counselor sided with me during our sessions, he refused to go anymore.

Our relationship was gradually getting worse. Raj was irritated all the time, and nothing could please him. I felt torn between work and home. I couldn't trust my husband and daughter to be in the same house without fighting. Natasha even threatened to run away if I didn't leave him.

"You have to take a step back, or you're going to lose the girl," I said to Raj one evening. "If I have to choose between you two, I will choose her. She means more to me."

It hurt me to say it, but it was the absolute truth.

Shortly after that, Raj and I separated. It was like a breath of fresh air for the girls and me, but it didn't solve as much as I had hoped.

అఅఅ

"How are things at home, Sunita?"

I swung my purse over my shoulder and met my friend Mary's compassionate eyes. Not only was she my co-worker, but she was also from India, and she had become my closest friend.

"I am okay," I answered, as we walked out of the hospital and were greeted by the heavy, sweet-smelling air of a typical Texas morning. "Things aren't quite as tense, I guess."

Mary nodded in silence as we continued toward our cars. For a couple of years, she had listened to me complain about life with Raj and pour out my heart about my parenting troubles. She was the only person I talked to about what was going on at home.

In turn, she shared with me her Christian faith, though I made it clear to her that I believed only that Jesus was a good man. I liked him the same as I liked Buddha or Gandhi.

"Would you like to come to church on Sunday?" she asked. She and her husband, Jacob, held church in their home. I knew this because she invited me to church almost every week, and every week I turned her down.

"Thank you, no," I said, shaking my head. "But you can pray for me."

"I always do," Mary answered with a smile.

We waved goodbye and climbed into our cars.

❦❦❦

A few months after Raj and I separated, I learned that he had been going to Jacob and Mary's house for church on Sundays. I also heard that he had become a Christian. I wanted to laugh; I had known Raj for 17 years, and it seemed completely out of character for him. But I respected Jacob and Mary for trying to help.

After 10 months apart, we decided to try to live together again. Raj did seem better — not perfect, but less angry overall.

"I have one condition," I told him. "I respect your beliefs, but I do not want you to talk to the girls and me about Jesus."

"Okay," he agreed.

I was a little irritated by his sudden church involvement. For the next two years, he went to prayer services on Saturday nights and church on Sunday mornings. He read the Bible frequently. But I figured that if he was busy with his Jesus, then he wasn't bothering me and the girls. And that was a positive thing.

Pastor Jacob and Mary became close family friends. I felt that Pastor Jacob was a wonderful person and that he was having a good influence on Raj. As long as I didn't have to listen to their religious discussions, I was fine.

ॐॐॐ

"This would look pretty on you, Jasmine," I said, holding up a purple skirt for her to see.

"Oh, that's lovely!" she agreed, her face breaking into a

broad smile. I double-checked the size, then placed the skirt into the cart for Jasmine to try on later. We were accumulating quite a pile of clothing.

"Mom! Look! That's my friend Emily from school!"

Before I could respond, Jasmine was darting across the store on her way to greet her friend. Emily reacted with equal enthusiasm, and her mom smiled warmly and waved at me.

"Come meet my mother," Jasmine was saying, leading them toward me, and soon we were exchanging names and phone numbers.

Emily's mother, Angela, was the happiest person I think I'd ever met. She was so personable, and she seemed to bubble over with energy and laughter.

She's probably never had tough times, I thought. I was envious of her easy smile and lightheartedness.

Pastor Jacob and Mary were coming over for dinner later that week, so I decided to invite Angela and her family, too. It would be nice to make more friends.

As it turned out, Angela was a single mom, and she brought Emily and her son, Dustin.

"These are our dear friends Pastor Jacob and Mary," I said, as everyone shook hands in our front entryway. "And Raj and I are actually celebrating our 20th wedding anniversary tonight."

"Oh, congratulations!" Angela beamed. "That's great!"

Conversation came easily over dinner. Raj and I sat at either end of the dining room table, our daughters and friends squeezed in elbow to elbow, all of us chatting as we ate. Every now and then, Angela's beautiful laugh would ring out, and we'd all chuckle along. Her joy was contagious.

"I'm so happy to be a part of your anniversary celebration," Angela said, turning to Raj and me. "It's all because of Jesus! He is the source of your marriage — the one who makes it a success."

Our friends nodded their agreement. "Thank you, Jesus."

Angela, too? Must all my friends be Christians?

Angela went on to share her life story — the troubles she had faced and how she had gone through a broken marriage and emerged stronger. She shared how she became a believer in Jesus, was able to start her own business and how she raised her kids on her own with God's help. It was an impressive story. She *had* been through tough times, yet she seemed so happy in spite of it all. I watched her eyes shine as she talked, and I wished with all my heart that I had a faith like Angela's.

৵৵৵৵

I began spending a lot of time with Angela. She had such a positive outlook on life, and I hoped some of that optimism might rub off on my family and me.

"How do you do it?" I asked her. "You are so happy — laughing, joking. I am so stressed out!"

"I have Jesus," Angela replied simply. "He helps me!"

"I wish I had your faith."

"But you can!"

"No," I said. "How can I have faith blindly? I can't believe in something I can't see."

"That's faith," she answered, an amused smile playing about her lips.

I loved my new friend, but she irritated me with the vagueness of her Christian faith. I had seen its amazing results in her life, but my scientific mind couldn't comprehend how it worked.

Natasha had graduated from high school and was set to go to Texas State University in the fall, 40 miles away from home. True to her word, she had stopped taking her medication when she turned 18, and now she was nervous and depressed all the time. She wasn't sure she wanted to go to college after all.

"I am so stressed out about Natasha," I told Angela one day in late July. "She is so anxious about starting school. She struggles with heavy depression, and I don't know what to do to help."

"Maybe I can try talking to her," Angela suggested.

I figured it was certainly worth a try. Natasha liked Angela, just like I did.

So Angela started coming over, but instead of encouraging Natasha to go to college, she talked to her about Jesus, which bothered me. My daughter had a strong and spunky personality, and she wasn't about to be swayed into anything.

"I know. I like Jesus! He sacrificed his life. But I don't think he's God," she'd argue.

The discussions went on for a couple of weeks. Angela would sit in our living room, talking freely about her faith, while I sat quietly and listened and watched Natasha get worked up.

I wanted to believe in it so badly, but my mind was fighting it. I had seen the change in Raj's heart. I had seen the light in Angela's face. I had seen the gentleness and patience in Pastor Jacob and Mary's friendship. But believing in Jesus would go against everything I believed about science.

What's happened to your science now?

I had been a quiet observer up to this point, refusing to get involved, refusing to argue semantics. But suddenly, in the middle of the conversation, I felt like someone pushed me from behind, and the questions I had been mulling over in my head tumbled out of my mouth before I could stop them — questions about the Christian belief that Jesus, God's son, had been raised from the dead. To me, that was the most difficult story to explain. How could someone who had been declared dead suddenly have life again? I needed answers that would prove that he really was God.

Angela seemed surprised by my outburst but patiently answered my questions one at a time.

"No, I don't believe in it," Natasha said, tears streaming down her face. She stood to her feet and walked out of the room.

I sighed heavily. This was not what I had wanted. I feared that all of these religious conversations were making Natasha worse. My friend and I sat in silence for a minute, and I could hear the ticking of the clock on the living room wall.

"Sunita," she finally said, gently, "it takes more faith to believe in some of what science says than to believe in God."

"You're asking me to have faith, but I don't know how!" I could tell that my irritation and frustration were showing through in my voice.

"Okay. I'll tell you what. Start reading the Bible. Read it every day for three weeks. Read the Gospel of John, and at the end of three weeks, we will continue the discussion."

"All right." I nodded, a little curtly. I was tired of arguing.

༄༄༄

Over the next few days, I did read the Gospel of John. I used Raj's Bible and flipped through the worn pages, drinking in the stories about Jesus — his teachings, his miracles, his willingness to die and take the punishment for all the ugly things we had done. Then, the part that most intrigued me — how he came back to life. When I was reading the Bible, the darkness I felt in my heart seemed to temporarily fade away.

Natasha approached me one evening as I was doing some work in the dining room.

"Mom?"

"Yes, darling?"

She looked down at the carpet, as if trying to decide which words to use.

"I want to go to church with Angela. But I want you to come with me."

"You can go," I replied. After all, Jasmine had gone with them before and loved it.

"No, I want you to come."

"No, sweetie, I don't think so." I sighed and shook my head.

"Mom, do you remember last week when Angela was talking to us, and I was crying?"

How could I forget?

"Well, that night I was feeling worse. I didn't want to live anymore." She paused. "I was thinking, *If there is a God, please help me.* And I ached in my heart. As I lay in bed, Jesus came to my mind, and I saw his face. A peace came over me, and I slept soundly that night."

A chill passed through me as I stood there, looking into my daughter's earnest face. I was a little jealous; I wished I could experience a moment like that in my life — a moment that would put all my questions to rest once and for all.

"Okay. I will go if it will help you. I will do anything to help you." I meant every word. I would do whatever it took to help free my daughter from the cloud of darkness that hovered.

"Great! Thanks, Mom!" And then my Natasha smiled — a rare wide, beautiful smile.

NO GOING BACK

࿇࿇࿇

The next Sunday, the girls and I joined Angela and her kids at Freedom Church. From the moment we entered the building, we were overwhelmed by loving, smiling people.

"Welcome!"

"Good morning!"

"God bless you!"

They seemed genuinely happy that we were there — as if they'd known us for ages. The atmosphere was festive and happy, unlike anything I had seen before. I felt welcomed and loved.

When the pastor gave the message, I couldn't believe how much the words he spoke seemed to be meant for me. He was answering all my questions — all the ones that had been brewing in my mind for months and years.

How does he know?

When the church service was over, I felt like I was smiling from ear to ear.

"I want to come back next week," I said to Angela.

And I did. I couldn't wait for Sundays to come around. I loved the songs in the worship service, but even more, I looked forward to hearing Pastor Benito's message. As he preached, Jasmine and I would look at each other, our mouths open in astonishment.

"That is the answer to our question yesterday!" we'd whisper to one another. It was like God was answering all of our questions through the pastor.

I continued to read through the Gospel of John, and I began to believe that what was written there was true. When I was done with John, I moved on to the rest of the Bible. I wanted to read it all at once; I couldn't get enough. When I wasn't reading the Bible, I was thinking about it. Raj and I even set up a meeting with Pastor Benito so I could ask him additional questions I came up with as I read.

Is this really happening? I used to tease people about becoming Christians!

I worried that my family might disown me if they found out. But I kept reminding myself of the one thing I knew for sure: My life had changed the moment I walked into that church. That was the truth! How could I say no to the truth?

৵৵৵

Nobody was happier to hear that the girls and I were going to church than Mary and Pastor Jacob. In late August, as Natasha prepared to move to college, Pastor Jacob asked if he and Mary could come over and pray for her.

We were standing in a circle, holding hands in our living room, when Pastor Jacob looked at Natasha and me and asked, "Would you like to accept Jesus as your Savior?"

The question caught me off guard.

Well, yes, I guess I believe in Jesus, but —

I felt confused. My mind was a whirlwind of all the reading I had done and the church services I had attended in the previous four weeks. I had learned so much. But this was the moment of truth. This is when I had to decide if a relationship with Jesus was the answer to the restlessness in my heart. I had to decide that Jesus was more than simply a good man, as I had always believed. I had to know that he truly was my Savior and that he had died to pay for the things I'd done wrong. I was drawn to Jesus by his love.

"Yes," I answered, raising my chin decisively.

My eyes locked with Natasha's, and she nodded.

"Yes."

Pastor Jacob put his hands on our heads then and prayed with us.

"If you accept Jesus, raise your hand and say it," he instructed.

We did. Relief flooded my body, and I knew in my heart that I was a child of God.

Raj embraced me, tears streaming down his cheeks and landing in his graying goatee.

"Oh, I am so relieved!" he said. "I am so happy!"

It took me 51 long years, but I finally admitted I couldn't do it on my own. I needed the one who *created* science to save me from myself and to guide my life. My eyes welled with tears as I felt the peace and love of Jesus surrounding me. And I knew that nobody would ever love me as much as he did.

FREEDOM STORIES

❧❧❧

Life wasn't perfect after that. But there was finally peace in my heart so that I could deal with the imperfections. The darkness over our home lifted, and the stress wasn't overwhelming. Natasha had a few ups and downs, but she was feeling so much better overall, and she turned to our pastors with her many questions. Her heart was softened, and instead of shouting that she hated us, she frequently told us she loved us.

Raj really liked attending Pastor Jacob's church because he had mentored him and spoke our native language. The girls and I really enjoyed Freedom Church because of Pastor Benito's wonderful messages and the happy social atmosphere. So we decided to compromise. We'd attend Pastor Jacob's 9 a.m. service and still have time to be at Freedom Church for the 11 a.m. service. It worked out wonderfully.

At home, we started having a family prayer time together every night at 9. Natasha faithfully reminded us if we forgot. We ate at the table as a family, too, which we hadn't done in a very long time.

I dug into the Bible with even more fervor than before. I was astonished that even though it was written hundreds and hundreds of years ago, it was still applicable today. Every time I read it, I learned something new. It was like a book of law, except that it was "living," and it gave me the wisdom I needed, hour by hour.

NO GOING BACK

❧❧❧

"You are more beautiful now than you have ever been," Raj said, bending down to kiss my face, love and gentleness in his eyes.

I felt a nervous flutter in my heart and the heat rising to my cheeks. Compliments from Raj had always been rare, as was any type of affection. I couldn't remember the last time he'd kissed me.

Raj's and my marriage had improved tremendously, and we were finally experiencing some unity for the first time in our 20 years together. He seemed to be a completely different person than the troubled, depressed man I had married, and I knew he felt the same way about me. But it wasn't our doing. It was Jesus in us who had softened our stubborn, hardened hearts and filled us with his love.

❧❧❧

Six months after becoming a Christian, I learned that my brother Satish was in poor health, so I returned home to India for three weeks. Even though it was stressful and scary, I knew in my heart that everything was going to be okay.

My parents had long since passed away, but I had several opportunities to share my new faith in Jesus with my siblings, which was important to me. All of them were still Hindus.

"I don't go to temple anymore," I told my older sister one day when she invited me to go with her to the temple. "I go to church and worship Jesus."

"Oh, Sunita, don't tell Satish!" she warned. "That will not make him happy."

I understood that she was afraid the news would shock him and worsen his health, and I couldn't help but be a little worried that he and the others might indeed be angry. But there was no shame in the truth. I knew that it was God's desire to reach each of them, too, in his timing. Jesus had changed my life, and he could do the same for them. It was good news that deserved to be shared.

When I told my story to Satish's wife, she said, "My sister also is a Christian. I have been trying to talk her out of it."

"Oh, no." I smiled, knowingly. "Don't try to talk her out of it. She is changed. There is no going back for her now."

My brother recovered, and I thanked God for healing him and sparing his life. And when I finally had a chance to open up to him about the change Jesus had made in me, he was surprisingly supportive.

"Isn't that what our father taught us?" Satish said. "It doesn't matter. I respect what you believe."

I breathed a sigh of relief and a prayer of thankfulness to God. It was a satisfying conclusion to my trip, to know that I had boldly shared the truth with my family. I believed that God would continue to work on their hearts, just as he had worked on mine.

NO GOING BACK

కొకొకొ

As I boarded the plane back to the United States, I thought back to that day that I jumped into Angela and Natasha's conversation in the living room. I was still amazed that I had done that at all. It was completely unlike me to take part in religious discussions and debates.

What if I hadn't? What if I'd just sat there, content to let my questions go unanswered? Where would I be today?

I knew the answer. I knew that I would still be stressed out about my life, bitter at Raj, anxious about Natasha and living in the same cloud of darkness and depression, one ugly day rolling into the next. But instead, I now had hope and peace. Raj and I were better than ever, and I trusted God to give my daughters the peace they needed, too. I woke up each morning with joy that couldn't be explained.

I believed that it was Jesus himself who pushed me from behind that day, who prompted me to voice the unspoken questions that plagued my brain. He wanted me to get the answers I sought. He wanted me to know his love.

My plane lifted off the ground of my homeland and high into the sky, heading toward Texas, heading toward home and the happy and peaceful future ahead. My heart skipped a beat with the excitement I felt to be reunited with my girls and Raj. I was even excited to see my two cats, Belle and Dove. I watched the earth gradually disappear from view as we entered the clouds and then gradually broke free, soaring above them. It was symbolic of my life and what Jesus had done for me.

And I remembered my words to my sister-in-law.

There's no going back.

FREE TO SOAR
The Story of Elaina
Written by Angela Welch Prusia

The flash of some distant memory blinded me.

I blinked, taking in my surroundings. A baby smiled across the restaurant, her pudgy hand holding a cracker. Her parents cooed over her antics, completely unaware of my suffocation.

My chest tightened with the familiar ache. Their joy triggered my deepest pain. I reached for my water glass, hands trembling.

"Are you okay?" A deep voice broke my trance. The dark thoughts crept back into the deep recesses of my mind.

"I'm fine." I managed a weak smile. The lie settled at the back of my throat like vomit.

He reached across the table to lace his fingers with mine. I recoiled at his touch. Doesn't he see the real me?

I'm so unworthy of love.

I couldn't let myself remember.

If I did, the tears would never stop …

ๅๅๅ

"Wait outside," Mama told me. "We'll just be a minute." She and her boyfriend, Sam, disappeared into

18D, the apartment in the housing projects in Lower Manhattan where his parents lived. Cinderblock walls felt like a tomb around me. The smell of urine drifted from the elevator doors.

Angry voices penetrated the paper-thin walls. I squeezed my eyes shut and tried to think happy thoughts. Swinging at the park. Or smelling bouquets of flowers.

"I don't want some divorcee and her b****** child in my home." The words rose above the others and struck my heart.

Mama marched out of the apartment trailed by Sam. Tears stained her face.

The door swung on its hinges, framing an angry woman. She scowled at me until I turned and fled after my mother.

Mama had been so happy since she'd met Sam, I couldn't bear the thought of her losing another man. Life hadn't been easy on Mama since she left Cuba as a young mother without the support of my father. If my soon-to-be grandmother didn't like me, I decided, then I would be so good that she would have to love us.

If only it was that easy.

No matter how hard I tried, the woman showed no affection toward me. I might as well have been invisible to her. I had to sneak food out of the kitchen when I was hungry. She never paid any attention to me.

"Come watch TV with me," Grandpa called out. His attention filled the emptiness inside.

My grandmother scowled at me from across the

apartment. At best, the two tolerated each other. At night, they slept in separate rooms.

My mom and Sam, by then her new husband, were engrossed in each other, so I jumped on Grandpa's bed and leaned against him. *The Ten Commandments* played on the television screen. Pharaoh kissed his wife, mesmerizing me.

"Let's act out the scene." I jumped up. "I'll cover my mouth with my hand, and you can kiss me."

Something glinted in Grandpa's eye. "You don't have to use your hand."

Before I realized what was happening, he kissed me boldly on the mouth, even with the rest of the family in the house for the Easter holiday. Shame filled me. Just like the time my babysitter's husband molested me.

My 6-year-old mind couldn't distinguish the desire for attention with my horror and shame. Terrified, I said nothing about what either man had done.

Grandpa's behavior got bolder, worsening until I turned 12 and finally mustered enough courage to threaten him. "If you touch me again, I'll kill you."

I swore to myself that life would be different.

৵৵৵

No matter how hard I tried not to, I seemed to attract predators like a magnet. The summer I turned 14, I was hanging out with the neighbor kids when things quickly got out of control. I went with an older boy upstairs to his family's apartment to use the bathroom. He had other intentions. He turned off the lights, pushed me down on the bed and raped me.

Shame left me defeated and powerless.

"You're not going to tell anyone, right?" I begged. I felt so dirty.

"Of course not," Daniel swore.

I never told my awful secret, pretending instead that the incident never happened.

A year later, it came back to haunt me. My boyfriend, John, complained to his teammates on the football team that I refused to sleep with him.

"Elaina?" Daniel sneered. "She's not a virgin. The little ho did me."

John cornered me in his house after the game. "Why'd you lie to me?"

"What are you talking about?" I ran a finger down his arm in an effort to distract him.

"Daniel told me all about your little fling. How many other guys have you slept with?"

My blood turned cold. "He's lying. Daniel raped me."

John's temple throbbed. "That's not what he said."

John refused to listen. Instead of dumping him, I got sucked into his pleas. "Come on, baby. I love you. You love me. Why not make it official?"

I hated the thought of losing John, so I finally agreed. I got pregnant at age 15.

తతత

"John, we gotta talk." I wrung my hands.

He kissed my ear. "What's up, babe?"

I told him the news.

The color drained from his face. "We gotta take care of this. We're not ready for a kid."

I didn't know what to say. John was right. *How could I support a baby?* I still had two years of high school to finish.

I made an appointment the next week.

The abortion clinic looked like my dentist's office. I dismissed my nerves and put on a phony front. No one counseled me on other options. My tears brought me no compassion from the nurses and doctor.

Like after the rape, I left the office pretending nothing happened. I ate lunch and went home to sleep. I didn't tell anyone my awful secret. It was easier to lie to myself than face the disgrace.

My abortion seemed to kill all life around me. Hate rooted itself inside my heart.

John and I continued to see each other for a while. It wasn't long before we broke it off.

I swore to myself that I would be stronger next time. Instead, I found myself in another unhealthy relationship, this time with a drug dealer. I longed for love. Instead, I fell for the empty promises of a dealer who only loved what I could give him in bed.

I cried when the pregnancy test came back positive. My boyfriend didn't have to speak. His eyes said everything.

Alone and afraid, I drove to the women's clinic.

"I don't want to do this!" I told the nurse. "Is this my only choice?"

She patted my hand. "Honey, do you have a job?"

I shook my head.

"Then how are you going to take care of a baby?" She told me to lie down. "You have your whole life in front of you."

Her words brought little comfort. I couldn't stop crying when I left the office.

My boyfriend was too wrapped up in his desires and drug deals to notice my despondency.

My third pregnancy followed the same pattern. Desperation for love warred with my feelings of unworthiness. Poor judgment blinded me.

I couldn't quit sobbing at the clinic. The doctor ended my baby's life, while the nurse screamed at the anesthesiologist for not subduing me.

I hated myself.

࿐࿐࿐

My mom and Sam divorced during my senior year of high school. I pretended not to care, but inside I was miserable. I tried to drown the pain in drugs. At my graduation from the all-girls' Catholic school, I stared across the Gothic cathedral to the nearly empty row where my mother and great aunt sat. The divorce left us without the large extended family I'd always known.

FREE TO SOAR

I worked as a dental assistant before I met my first husband. I longed for a normal guy after my breakup with the drug dealer, but Collin loved money more than me. His late hours only compounded my issues with intimacy. We lasted less than a year.

My second marriage left me frustrated. I was attracted to my husband's Jewish faith. But the more I tried to practice his religious traditions, the more he broke the rules. I got irritated with his total disregard for his spiritual heritage. His drinking problem widened the gap between us until I severed it entirely by initiating my second divorce.

I moved to San Francisco full of remorse. Alone, I turned inward. I knew about Jesus from my Catholic education, but I longed for a deeper connection with God.

I had no intention of falling in love when I met Roberto. Despite his own failed relationships, his faith in God appealed to me, and we began attending church together.

As I listened to the preacher talk about the Bible, I realized that not all spiritual paths lead to eternal life. Only the cross paved the way to the one true God. Jesus didn't care for my empty religious rituals. He wanted a personal relationship with me.

"I need you, Jesus!" I cried out one Sunday. "Help me to change."

My heart of stone began to crumble.

I was a mess. Jesus had a lot of work to do.

ৡৡৡ

God's standard for abstinence wasn't easy for me given my old patterns. When I found out I was pregnant, the news overwhelmed me. I feared I'd lost my chance at motherhood after my abortions. I wanted to raise this baby with his father. Roberto and I had fallen in love and had set a wedding date, but after I found out I was pregnant, any doubts I might still have had melted away, and we decided to get married sooner.

God, in his infinite mercy, blessed me with a healthy pregnancy and a beautiful delivery. When the nurse handed me my son, the recognition was instant. Tomas' little face, even his cry, were familiar. I felt as if I'd known him my whole life.

Roberto and I hit a rough patch in our marriage. I wanted to run like in the past, but this time, I had to think about my son. Trust took some time to rebuild, but Roberto and I renewed our commitment to stay together. God blessed us with another son, Carlo, the following year.

Being a mother brought fulfillment to my very core. The gift was the most precious of treasures, and I viewed them as a sign of God's assurance of love for me. Even now as my sons approach school age, I gaze at them and see the human personification of God's forgiveness.

ৡৡৡ

A job opportunity took our family to Spain, but it fell apart, and after five months without a paycheck, we depleted our savings. We were immigrants without resources in a foreign country.

"It's time to move back to the States," Roberto told me.

My heart sank when neither one of us could find a job in California near any of our family. We decided to move back in with my parents.

Our stress compounded when I learned we were expecting another baby.

"I'm pregnant," I told Roberto that night. "What are we going to do?"

"Have faith," he said, but his eyes betrayed his fears.

I refused to have another abortion. Instead, I spent my birthday at the welfare office because we didn't have medical insurance.

Five weeks later, I miscarried our baby. My heart broke.

Things seemed to be getting grimmer as the weeks turned to months.

As I lay on an air mattress in my husband's arms, he whispered in my ear, "What are we going to do? We're drowning."

We decided to trust God. We believed he would provide for us, as he always had.

A few days later, a friend posted a job opportunity on Facebook.

I couldn't type a reply fast enough. "I'll take it."

"You're willing to move to Texas?" she replied back.

"Uh, sure." I hadn't realized the job meant a move, but I accepted the position, anyway. Fifteen days later, we were in Texas.

తతత

As I began to study the Bible for the first time, I struggled with forgiving my step-grandfather. I couldn't believe that God viewed all sin equally. My step-grandfather stole my innocence. *How could a gracious God forgive child molesters?*

"Listen to this." I read from the first chapter of Romans to Roberto one night. "Since they didn't think it was worthwhile to acknowledge God, God abandoned them to a defective mind to do inappropriate things."

Roberto climbed into bed while I continued to build my case.

I tapped the Bible. "This proves what I've been saying. God doesn't forgive all sin."

Roberto started to disagree, but he was patient and knew I would have to choose to forgive in my own time. I didn't ask our pastor for his counsel because the last time I'd talked to a Catholic priest about forgiveness, I felt like he'd judged me. After that, I didn't feel like anyone could forgive me. I definitely didn't want to forgive my perpetrator.

I felt God nudge me. *Start praying for your grandpa. You have to forgive him.*

Ignoring God didn't work.

"Okay, God." I closed my eyes. "Thank you that he's dead."

Try again. I could almost see God cross his arms in challenge.

"Then you're going to have to help me." I frowned. "If I'm going to forgive him, I don't want to pretend. I want this at my core."

The day before we left for Texas, my mom and I were shopping when my brother called.

"I'm here with Dad," Alonso said. "He wants to see you."

I paled. After my parents' divorce, my stepdad had been arrested for selling cocaine to a police officer. I was too angry to visit him in prison. I'd seen him only a handful of times in the previous two decades.

"What's wrong?" Mom whispered.

"Dad wants to see me." I gulped.

The blood rushed from her face. I agreed to visit.

My dad walked into the food court at the mall 15 minutes later. Immediately, I saw the arrogant man had been replaced by a different, softer version. Christ immediately softened my heart. Suddenly I remembered the good moments. My stepdad had been there for my growing-up years. I knew he had done the best he could.

My mom watched the boys, while we talked for a short time. I didn't feel comfortable being totally open with him, but we exchanged contact information and promised to reach out and keep in touch.

During one of our subsequent phone conversations,

after catching up on family news, I broached the subject of my grandfather. The last time I'd seen my stepdad had been at a family therapy session, where my brother confided some painful memories about being molested by our grandfather.

"I'm not really over what Grandpa did to me," I confessed.

"What do you mean?" Sam asked, sounding confused.

"Grandpa molested me for six years."

"What?" My stepdad broke down, stunned and horrified. "I didn't know."

"You don't remember me talking about it at the therapy office?"

Guilt washed over Sam. "I must've been so traumatized with everything we talked about during therapy. I'm so sorry."

Relief made me relax. He was sorry. He deeply cared. In that moment, my white horse reared up, and my prince stepped in to rescue me.

"I wish I could kill him," Sam seethed. "I'd go dig up his grave and kill him again. I feel so awful."

I longed to hug him through the phone. His words erased the estranged years. Tears glistened in my eyes.

"My father's a monster. People will think I'm just the same."

I shook my head. "You're not him. I'm sorry I never visited you in prison."

He gulped. "Thank you."

"I've started praying for him."

"Really?" Sam gasped. "My dad asked for forgiveness on his deathbed."

It was my turn to gasp. "Are you serious?"

"Grandpa couldn't speak. He had a stroke," Sam explained. "But he grasped for a piece of paper and wrote, 'I'm sorry for everything I've done.'"

Waves of astonishment washed over me. I'd never expected forgiveness was possible for my abuser.

అ అ అ

Our move to Texas turned out to be exactly what we needed. Roberto got a job soon after we settled into our home.

He and Tomas went to the park for an Independence Day celebration, while I stayed home with Carlo, who was sick.

"We got ice pops," Tomas told me when they returned.

"Freedom Church was doing an outreach at the park," Roberto explained. "We should check them out on Sunday."

The storefront where Freedom Church met was different than the more formal Catholic cathedrals I'd attended. When we stepped inside, we immediately felt welcome. Pastor Benito's message spoke directly to both of us, so we began attending regularly.

A few months later, God shook me through a sermon.

"When we stand before the throne of God," Pastor

Benito said, "forgiveness won't be ours if we hold forgiveness back from others."

I shuddered at the thought. I want to meet my babies in heaven.

What if unforgiveness holds me back?

Pastor Ben continued by pointing out the very verse I had misinterpreted years before. "The only unforgiveable sin is the person who turns from God and refuses to ask for forgiveness."

Understanding finally hit. I'd held myself above others, regarding my abuse as a badge of pain. I needed forgiveness as much as my step-grandfather.

A post on Facebook caught my attention a few days later. I clicked on the link and listened to the speech of an eloquent 30-year-old woman with cerebral palsy. A survivor of a late-term abortion herself, she made an appeal to the authorities of Australia to ban late-term abortions.

"I'm an abortion survivor." Her words took the breath from me. "My mother didn't want me. But I'm here because I'm God's girl."

I blinked at the screen.

I killed my children. The gravity of my sin shook me to my core. I'd lied to myself for years, pretending that I didn't really have a choice. But I did, and I chose convenience. Women may have the right to make choices, but we also have the privilege to bear life.

I forgive you.

"How can you love me, God? I'm a sham, a liar."

That's why I died for you.

"I can't pretend anymore. How am I going to confess this, God?"

I became obsessed with pro-life videos. Day after day, I watched them, wailing to the depths of my soul for the children I longed to hold. I begged their forgiveness.

Mommy is so sorry, babies. Will you ever forgive me?

ॐ ॐ ॐ

I needed to talk to someone, but terror kept me silent. *What would people think of me?* With friends, I shared a post of a woman who'd given birth to a stillborn baby. As we cried together, my story stalled on my lips.

I opened my mouth, ready to share, and yet I couldn't.

You are a worthless excuse for a Christian. You can't share your story in front of the pastor's wife.

The old doubts pulled me into familiar darkness, and I lost my nerve.

Not long after, a friend caught me off guard with a phone call.

"Sorry to call so late, Elaina," Paige breathed into the receiver. "But I just wanted to tell you the details about our grow group."

I cocked my head. "Grow group?"

"The one you signed up for at church."

"There must be a mistake," I said. "I don't have time with work and the kids."

Eight weeks later, I was asked again to be a part of a

group. I knew I didn't have a lot of time to spend with other women in the church, but this time, I felt that I was supposed to be a part of it.

かかか

The six of us came from different backgrounds, but somehow we women fit together. I shared a very watered-down version of my story with them.

The next week one of the women gave such a raw testimony of her life, words gushed out of my mouth.

"I'm such a liar." I couldn't breathe. "My testimony is a big fat lie."

I broke down and told them everything. All the ugly, rotten details of my sordid past. When I finished the last word, I felt so devastated. Despicable. Unmasked.

I stared at my nails, afraid to see the condemnation I expected.

Instead, arms wrapped around me. Kindness and compassion embraced me.

It was time to stop pretending.

I shared my story with Pastor Benito, and he prayed for God to give me boldness. A few weeks later, I poured out my heart on videotape for our congregation. As the video played, I knew that God was using me to speak to others going through the same things.

Forgiveness set me free. Breaking the silence made me soar.

FREE TO SOAR

❧ ❧ ❧

A cascade of sunrays bathes my daughter in translucent light. Ebony eyes dance with joy. A chain of daisies crowns her curly head. She runs barefoot through a field of wildflowers, chasing after a butterfly. Laughter trails after her.

Her sister sits amidst the grass, the long blades nearly camouflaging her. Little fingers pluck petals from a prairie rose. A ladybug crawls up the stem and across her hand. She smiles as its wings lift, and the ladybug flits around her head.

The boys lay on their backs, staring into a blue sky wisped with clouds. The older one raises his hand and points out a dragon. He spears the tail with a pussy willow stick. His brother boards a cloudy pirate ship in search of treasure.

Even though I've never met my babies, I sense them like I knew Tomas and Carlo before I gave them birth. My babies live with God in heaven. I can't wait for the day I'll smother each one in kisses. I'll count their little fingers and tickle their toes.

My spirit longs for the ordinary, everyday things I can't reclaim on earth. I don't push away the memories like I once did whenever I saw a baby. Jesus has taken the sting from my past.

He waits for me in heaven with all four of my babies.

One day we'll celebrate birthdays and dandelion wishes, making mud pies and blowing bubbles, catching tadpoles and fireflies. We'll sleep under a galaxy of stars and dance in the rain. I'll hold my babies and feel their immortal hearts beat against mine.

An eternity awaits.

The anticipation makes me soar.

For readers (male or female) suffering from abortion trauma, please contact your local Christian pregnancy center [(512) 248-8200 in Round Rock] to find out about Bible study groups for post-abortion healing.

THE KID IN BLACK
The Story of Trevor
Written by Karen Koczwara

We could have killed her.

As I writhed in pain on the narrow bench inside the ambulance, an injured woman lay just a few feet away. A woman we almost killed.

My stomach twisted as the horrific accident unfolded again in my mind. The screeching metal, the dazed look on my friend's face, the smell of fire, the blaring sirens, the frantic scramble to escape and then, after the adrenaline finally drained, the searing pain as I lay helpless on the side of the road.

We could have killed her.

Though we were all alive, I knew my nightmare was far from over. In fact, it had just begun …

❧❧❧❧

I was born in Fort Wayne, Indiana, in 1979. Six months after my birth, my family relocated to Grand Rapids, Michigan. My mother worked at a bank, while my father held a job as a sales manager for a box company. My parents tried church before I was born, but something happened there that hurt and disappointed them, so they decided not to raise me with religion. We struggled to make ends meet, and most of my clothes came from the

Goodwill and other secondhand stores. An annual back-to-school shopping trip with my grandparents became the highlight of my year.

As an only child, I was especially close with my father's parents. When Pop-pop, my maternal grandfather, passed away in 1991, I cried for a few minutes and then told myself I would never cry like that again. I donned a tough shell, which I managed to live beneath for many years, until my life completely fell apart.

School did not come easily for me. I struggled and did not learn to read well until the fifth grade. Things got even harder in middle school. I often felt bored and didn't bother to apply myself. I kept busy playing soccer until the eighth grade, when my knees gave me trouble and I turned in my cleats. I played the trumpet in the school band but gave that up as well. It wasn't long before trouble started to brew.

My grandparents lived just over the hill from our house, and on Christmas and Easter, I reluctantly joined them for church. They often talked about their faith in God, but I usually didn't pay much attention.

When I was 13, my interest in God piqued, and I began asking their pastor questions. He told me about a God who loved me, reading me passages out of the Bible. It all sounded nice, and I wondered if I might want a relationship with that God. As an only child with few friends and parents who both worked full time, I often felt lonely. Could this God he talked about fill some sort of void in my life?

THE KID IN BLACK

I continued to ponder these questions, but my excitement was soon squelched. I had long hair and often wore black, and kids at school began to dub me a devil worshipper. They spat hurtful words into my face, and I accepted the sting without fighting back. But inside, something shifted. *These kids say they love God, but look at them, judging me for being different. They don't even know me! You know what? If this is how Christians act, I don't want their God. Besides, we all die in the end, so what's the point in living?*

From that moment on, I decided to become an atheist and picked up cigarettes instead of a Bible. Smoking became my new pastime. Because I grew facial hair as a young adolescent, I looked older than my age. Convenience store clerks rarely carded me for cigarettes. Other kids approached me, asking me to buy them a pack, too. I hid my little secret from my parents, knowing they'd be disappointed if they found out.

Some close friends invited me to church one day, but I hastily turned them down. "No way! I am not setting foot in there!" I cried. I was done with church and done with God. Christians, as far as I was concerned, were nothing but a bunch of hypocrites. They could take their Bibles and their Jesus stuff. I didn't want anything to do with it.

My dad was tough and had high expectations of me. One day, I got angry at my mother and hurled a few cuss words at her. She got upset and told me I'd have to deal with my father when he got home. When he returned, we exchanged heated words. I went in to hit him, and he shouted, "Make it a good one, boy!" My fist made contact with his body, and a physical fight ensued. From then on, I knew he meant business.

When I was 15, my father started a new position at work and only came home on the weekends. My mother and I ate dinner alone, often struggling to make conversation. We lived as three separate entities. When I got my driver's license, it was my first taste of real freedom. What little family unity we'd maintained seemed to vanish the minute I got the keys to my own car.

"Be back by 9 p.m.!" my parents called out as I raced toward the car.

But I came home at 1 a.m. instead and found my parents still waiting up for me.

"Give me your keys," my father said sternly.

"Tough s***," I replied hotly. "You can have the keys, but you'll have to drive me to school and work and everywhere else I need to go."

They quickly changed their minds and let me off the hook.

I tried my first joint at 16 and enjoyed the high that hit a few minutes after the smoke reached my lungs. I began getting high before school, often sneaking in a joint or two after my early morning auto-body class. A few eye drops and a spritz of cologne disguised the smoke smell, and my teachers never caught on.

Auto-body class, part of an extracurricular vocational program, became the highlight of my week. Fast cars fascinated me. The faster the car, the better I liked it. But it was this love affair with speed that would soon land me in a heap of trouble.

By my junior year, I hated school. I had a few close friends, but I kept my distance from everyone else. The label "Devil Worshipper" had stayed with me throughout junior high and high school, and it stung. I tried to convince myself I didn't care, that I didn't need popularity or acceptance. But the rejection left a wound nonetheless. I looked forward to the day I never had to set foot on campus again.

School bored me, and despite taking a few challenging courses, I struggled to maintain interest. I continued getting high daily and began skipping class. After taking a test one day, I walked out of the room before the bell rang.

"Where are you going?" the teacher's shrill voice called after me.

"I'm leaving," I replied nonchalantly.

After I skipped almost an entire semester, my counselor grew concerned and threatened not to give me the credits for my classes. The principal called my mother to discuss my alarming behavior. But a couple of teachers spoke up on my behalf.

"This kid may not show up very often, but he gets great grades and aces most of his tests. He must just be bored," they concluded.

At last, the principal agreed to give me the credits.

The August before my senior year, I enlisted in the Marine Corps and entered the Delayed Entry Program, planning to head off to Basic Training after graduation.

Joining the Marines seemed a logical choice for a bored, troubled kid like me. I'd get to travel and see the world, enjoying the adventure I found only when I revved up a fast car and heard the motor purr.

I began my senior year with just four classes on campus and enrolled in computer programming courses at the local junior college, becoming one of the first students to participate in dual enrollment. By now, my teachers had figured out I was smart. The classes, coupled with my vocational tech program, kept me sane.

My parents discussed moving to Florida my senior year, and I jumped at the idea. "Let's go now!" I said, eager for a fresh start.

"No, you need to stick out school and graduate," they convinced me.

And so I hung on. But that Thanksgiving, my best friend called at 11 a.m., sobbing uncontrollably. "Alison's been in a car accident," he cried.

My stomach lurched. I'd grown close to his sister Alison and her three little girls over the years. The children had become the nieces I thought I'd never have, and they affectionately called me Uncle Trevor. "Is she okay?" I croaked, hardly able to get the words out. *Please, let her be okay.*

"She's all right."

Relief washed over me, but I sensed something was still wrong. I'd never heard my friend so out of control. "Was there anyone else in the car with her?" I dared to ask, sucking in my breath.

"The girls. They're all dead. All three of them." He sputtered the words between sobs.

No. This can't be right. I pictured the girls, just 9, 7 and 4 years old. *Those precious little girls, full of innocence and life.* It was too unbearable to think about.

For the first time since my grandfather's death, I couldn't hold back the tears. They came hard and fast, and I could not stop them. The girl's sweet faces danced in my mind, and I sobbed uncontrollably for them and the lives they'd never live out. The injustice was incomprehensible.

Now I know for sure. There isn't a God, because he would never allow such a thing to happen, I thought bitterly.

Though I'd claimed myself as an atheist for years, I'd always remembered that time in my grandparents' church and had still clung to a shred of hope that perhaps God really existed. But now I was sure. A loving God would never sit back and permit such a tragedy.

I soon learned the details of the horrific accident. Alison had been on her way home with her three girls just after a heavy snowstorm. The roads had been plowed, but she got caught in the slush, and her car spun and drifted toward oncoming traffic at 55 miles per hour. The girls died instantly in the crash.

I attended the funeral. A crowd of people assembled around the family, who were under a large tent as rain came pouring down. There was not a dry eye in the crowd. My friend's family invited me to sit with them, but I stood just outside the tent, grateful for the rain that hid the tears trickling down my cheeks. *I don't want them to see me crying. Real men don't cry.*

As Christmas neared, I grew more depressed. I could not stop thinking about Alison and her three precious girls she'd just lost. Life seemed meaningless, cruel even. What was the point of living? My parents seemed to me too absorbed in their own lives to care much about mine, and I had only a couple real friends. School was a bore and a waste of time. Perhaps I would be better off dead.

I wrote a suicide letter and decided to head out to my grandparents' condo on Lake Michigan. The lake was frozen over, and the waves had created huge mounds of ice around the shore. *It's the perfect place to kill myself,* I decided. *I'll just slit my wrists and lay down on the ground to die. When the ice melts, I'll be washed away into the lake, never to be seen again.*

I drove out to the lake and stepped out of the car, the snow crunching beneath my feet as the chilly wind whipped at my cheeks. The sun had started to drop behind the trees, and soon it would be pitch-black outside. I imagined how it would feel to die, to just float away from this earth into a dark abyss of nonexistence. I didn't believe in God, and I didn't believe in heaven, either. *I'll just disappear, as though I never breathed at all.*

But standing there in the cold, the blood still pumping through my veins, I could not go through with my plan. It wasn't that I suddenly found life worth living — I just wasn't sure I wanted to be dead quite yet. At last, I got back into the car and headed home.

THE KID IN BLACK

My parents, as I'd suspected, were frantically upset. "What were you thinking?" they cried, waving the suicide note in the air. "You scared us, Trevor!"

I shrugged, not too concerned with their feelings. *You guys are so absorbed in your own lives, I'm surprised you even noticed I was gone.*

Convinced I needed help, my parents took me to a psychiatrist. I liked him well enough. I shared my feelings, and he listened with concern.

"You know, Trevor, I think you are bottling your emotions," he told me bluntly. "What I mean is, you are like a glass bottle. You tried to close the bottle after the accident and shove all your emotions inside. But eventually, these emotions aren't going to fit. If you don't let yourself feel, they'll soon burst out."

Deep down, I knew he was right. I could not keep pushing my emotions aside. I was trying to be tough on the outside, but inside, I was crumbling. Still, I could not bring back Alison's three little girls. Life felt meaningless, and I wasn't sure I wanted to participate in it. I had come to a crossroads, and it was time to decide if I would make sense out of my broken mess or keep shoving the mess into my emotional bottle. I chose to shove them back in the bottle.

Life marched on. That April, my friend picked me up in his mother's brand-new Buick Riviera, and we decided to take the car for a spin before heading out to a party. As my friend stepped on the gas, we headed down a two-lane country road.

"Have you maxed this thing out yet?" I asked him.

"No." He glanced over, a mischievous look in his eye, and then gunned it. I watched the speedometer climb to 120 miles per hour, and adrenaline raced through my veins. *Now this is what I'm talkin' about!*

We whizzed by a cop, and I gulped hard. Even though I never wore a seatbelt since being able to drive, something inside of me said to put it on. We roared over a hill. *Oh, s***, there's a slower car in our lane.* Instead of slowing down, my friend decided to pass the car in our lane. He jerked into the other lane, and a pair of blaring headlights blinked back at us. He yanked the car back into our lane, suddenly unable to avoid the car he had just been trying to pass, and slammed into it. The deafening sound of scraping metal against metal shot through the air. The car we'd hit immediately lost control and rolled into the woods beside the road.

The driver-side airbag went off and hit my friend in the face. He flew back against his seat, looking dazed. Our car hobbled to a halt, and I sat there a moment, a different sort of adrenaline now pumping through my body. No one can quite prepare for an accident. There is no protocol, no guidebook for how one will react. I simply sat there in shock. And then, horror overwhelmed me as the smell of fire hit my nostrils. *The car is on fire!*

I sprang into action, frantically tugging on the passenger door. But it wouldn't budge. At last, I freed myself and my friend, and we both tumbled onto the side of the road through the driver-side door and lay in the gravel. In that instant, the adrenaline drained, and I realized I was in an immense amount of pain.

Sirens roared, and a cop car skidded to a halt. When I glanced up, an officer had his gun drawn and pointed at us. "What the f*** were you boys thinking? Do you have any idea how fast you were f****** going?" he cried.

"Oh, s***!" his partner suddenly yelled. "There's a car in the woods on fire!"

The cops raced off into the woods, and my heart jumped in my chest. *It isn't our car on fire — it's the other car! Oh, man. This is really, really bad.*

The next few minutes were a blur, as a parade of fire trucks and police cars raced to the scene. I heard the words "Jaws of Life," and again, my heart jumped. *There's someone in that car, and they can't get him or her out. What if we killed the person inside?*

At last, the emergency medical technicians returned to us. By now, excruciating pain shot through my entire body. They snapped a neck brace on me, unbuttoned my shirt and took a pair of scissors to my undershirt and pants before strapping me to the gurney and loading me into the ambulance. Every moment felt like hours as they situated me inside and assessed my vitals. And then, to my horror, they placed the injured woman from the other car beside me and began assessing her as well. To my relief, she appeared completely coherent and answered every question they fired at her.

"I don't think we need the helicopter after all," I heard someone say, and I breathed another sigh of relief.

Does this mean she's going to be okay?

The ambulance raced off to the emergency room, and I lay on the bench, writhing in pain and trying to piece together the events of the last terrible hour in my muddled mind. We arrived at the hospital, and the doctors proceeded to walk me through a series of X-rays and exercises to determine the state of my injuries. As the minutes ticked by, it suddenly hit me — *where are my parents?*

"Can someone call my parents, and let them know I've been in an accident?" I asked the doctors. They assured me they would.

As I lay on the bed, half naked and in pain, I glanced over at the clock on the wall and realized it was now the middle of the night. *Where are my parents?* I wondered again, my heart sinking. *Why haven't they come?*

At 6 a.m., my parents arrived at last.

"Why didn't you come?" I asked angrily.

"If it was serious, we would have come," they replied, nonchalantly. "We told the doctors to call us when you were ready to come home."

I stared at them, incredulous. *So you knew all this time and you didn't come? How could you do such a thing? Weren't you worried sick?* A new, deep sort of hurt seeped into my heart, promising to linger for a very long time. *I'm your only son! Didn't you want to make sure I was okay? What's wrong with you guys?*

I slowly recovered physically after the accident, but the emotional aftermath proved harder to overcome. My mind constantly snapped to the woman beside me in the ambulance. *We didn't kill her, but we could have. How could I have lived with myself if we took her life, just the way Alison's daughters' lives were taken in that awful car accident?* I shuddered, realizing how grateful I was for a different outcome. *Things could have been much, much worse.*

Not long after the accident, my mother and I sat down to dinner one night together. We were not especially close, and I knew she often wondered about my life outside the house. As I stirred my food around, she asked out of the blue, "Trevor, have you had sex?"

I glanced up at my mother, dumbfounded. I then took a deep breath. "Okay, Mom, you know what? I'm going to give you a pass and tell you everything right now. You can ask anything you want. I will not lie to you. To answer your question, yes, I've had sex."

"With whom?" she pressed, raising her brow.

I told her.

"Is that it?"

I shook my head. "No, there were more." I rattled off a few more names.

She nodded and stared at her plate. "Have you done drugs?"

"Yes. Pot, Ritalin, a few other prescription drugs." I kept my eyes trained on her, knowing full well what I divulged was shocking. *I'm not the person she thought I was.*

"Do you smoke?"

"Yes, Mom, I smoke."

I laid it all out, holding nothing back. *You asked, Mom. You wanted the truth, and I gave it to you. Sorry if it hurts.*

My mother nodded and then sadly looked away, trying to process my words. We continued stirring our food around on our plates, but neither of us was hungry anymore.

That spring, someone set off a pipe bomb in a trash can in the school hallway. The trash can and nearby lockers blew up, and everyone sprang into action, terrified the entire school might burst into flames as well. Later, the vice principal pulled me into his office to question me.

"Did you do it?" he asked, not wasting words.

I stared at him. "No. I am not that stupid. If I had done it, I would have done it right. I would have done it in a science classroom where everything would have blown up." I knew I was being a smart aleck, but I didn't care.

Why is everyone always assuming I'm the troublemaker around here? Just because I'm different doesn't make me a devil worshipper, and it doesn't make me a criminal, either!

I continued talking with my Marine recruiter and told him I'd been in a bad car accident. When I tried doing pull-ups, I could not quite get up to the bar.

"If we can just get you to Basic Training, you will be covered medically," he said. "Just keep working at getting your strength back."

But I had injured my shoulder, and despite my best

efforts, I could not do a single pull-up. I realized I might not be able to join the Marines if I did not pass the physical test. My recruiter continued to push my paperwork through. Meanwhile, my parents made plans for moving to Florida the minute I finished high school and left for Basic Training. *Everything has to work out. I don't have a plan B.*

In June, I graduated from high school, relieved to never set foot in that place again. At last, the big day arrived, and I prepared to leave for boot camp. As I got ready to board the plane, a pair of military police officers raced up to me in the terminal.

"Master Gunnery Sergeant Verdean needs to speak to you immediately!" one of them barked.

It was the news I'd been dreading. Despite my recruiter's best efforts, because I had not passed the physical test, I would not be allowed to join the Marines after all. In an instant, the only dream I'd ever had was taken away. My heart sank along with my hopes.

When I returned home, I discovered that my parents had sold everything we owned in an estate sale. Even my bed was gone!

"What did you guys do?" I cried, enraged as I glanced around the empty house.

"We told you we were moving to Florida as soon as you graduated and headed to boot camp," my mother replied with a shrug. "This is our plan. Sorry. You can sleep on an air mattress in the camper for now."

I was speechless. Nevertheless, I was determined. *I am*

not going to go with them! I will find a way to make it here on my own. I may not have a clue what to do now, but I'll figure something out.

I'd dreamed of shooting in the infantry, but everything was different now. In August, my parents moved to Florida, and I landed a contract job as a computer graphic artist for a large publishing company. I rented a small bedroom from an elderly couple for $175. When the elderly man's wife passed away, he asked me to leave, and I scrambled to find another place to live.

With no one to keep me in check, I got reckless. I began dealing drugs, primarily pot, and also began hustling for money at pool halls every night. I landed a second job at a help desk, answering phone calls. They wanted me to come on full time, but I knew I'd never pass the drug test. I politely declined.

I landed another job as a computer programmer at a mortgage company and enjoyed the work. But meanwhile, I dealt and did drugs regularly and often partied with underage kids. The more drugs I used, the more my work life suffered. After throwing down a bad attitude with my employer, they asked me to leave, and we parted ways.

Two years out of high school, my life hit rock bottom. I moved into the basement of my girlfriend's parents' house, but they eventually told me to leave. My girlfriend and I secured an apartment together but broke up shortly after settling in. I obtained another job as a Web developer for a new company but soon realized I had serious problems. *I know I'm reckless, but I don't know how to climb out of this mess. Where do I go from here? My parents are living it up in Florida, and I have no one but an uncle left here. Maybe I need to get out of Michigan once and for all.*

Desperate, I called my parents in Florida and asked if I could move in with them.

"You can, but under certain conditions," they said. "You need to quit drinking, and you need to enroll in school or find a job."

I agreed to their terms. In November, my mother flew up to help me clean my apartment and pack what few belongings I owned. I made the move to Florida, intending to leave Michigan and all my troubles behind. But it wasn't long before I found the same troubles again.

I moved into my parents' spare bedroom and bunked up on the futon. In January, I began classes at the local college, excited to work my way toward a computer science degree. On my first day of class, I met a guy named Jim, and we hit it off. I soon discovered he dealt drugs. Within no time, I began dealing with him.

My new friend quickly learned I was good at "slinging." He brought me in on some of his bigger deals, and we began selling ecstasy, cocaine and any other drugs we could get our hands on. I began smoking pot again and soon graduated to cocaine. The exhilarating high was unlike anything I'd ever experienced. Suddenly, nothing was off limits.

I turned 21 in March and began regularly going out to bars. The milestone birthday brought with it a feeling of empowerment. *I can do anything I want now! I'm legal!* I began staying out until 3 or 4 a.m. every night, often stumbling into class on just a couple hours of sleep. I managed to keep up with my studies, but my grades slipped. Life was starting to look a lot like Michigan again.

I landed a job as a computer programmer for a newspaper. It seemed like the perfect fit. The employer asked me to take a drug test, and I panicked.

I've never had to take a drug test before. I'm certain I won't pass. I just did a whole bunch of coke and pot an hour ago!

Having spent enough time in the illegal drug trade, I'd heard about guys who knew how to get around drug tests. A few bought other people's urine to pass the test. I decided to go the old-fashioned way and drank a gallon of water instead. To my utter shock, I received a phone call the next day. I had miraculously passed the test!

For the next few months, I managed to squeak by in school and keep up with my new job. From the hours of 8 a.m. to 5 p.m., I abstained from drinking or drugs, but the minute 5 p.m. hit, I went out to party. My drug dealer friend asked me to meet his supplier, and I knew I'd just obtained new status with him. Meeting a supplier was considered the highest honor in our underground industry.

I met Franco one night. Tall, with bulging biceps, he was even more intimidating than I'd expected. I soon learned he had contacts all over Florida and could get us anything we wanted. Franco was a big deal.

THE KID IN BLACK

"Jim vouched for you," Franco told me. "Anything you want, you give me a call." He then leaned in, his eyes boring into mine. "You ever turn on me, though, and I will kill you. Got that?"

I waited for a smile, hoping he was joking. But he just stared at me with those wild eyes. "Sure thing," I gulped.

My drinking and drug problem worsened. That summer, I met with my mother for lunch and confided in her that I'd begun using again. "I know I need to get away. Things are getting pretty bad. Maybe a trip back to Michigan would help clear my head," I told her solemnly.

"I'll help you get there if you promise to go to AA when you get back," she said.

I agreed and returned to Michigan for a while. But the minute I got back to Florida, I began using again. I spent all the money I earned on booze and drugs and struggled to pay my bills. From 5 p.m. to 3 a.m., I partied hard. On my lunch break, I often snuck away to down three or four beers. *My boss must know I have a problem. Maybe if I keep my performance up, she won't say anything.*

On September 11, 2001, I went to work as usual. I busied myself alongside the others in my department, while the newspaper reporters busied themselves on the other side of the building. Suddenly, one of my co-workers announced there'd been a plane crash. We all dashed into the newsroom just in time to see the second plane hit the Twin Towers. As the massive building began to crumble, we watched in horror. *We've been attacked by terrorists,* I realized instantly.

And then came my second thought. *There is definitely no God. A loving God would not allow all these innocent people to lose their lives.*

I went back to work, and a short time later, a guy in the office sent out an e-mail. "Make sure you get right with God, because you never know when it's your last day," he wrote. I sneered at his words.

"When you die, you just die and decompose in the ground," I told him as I rolled my eyes. *Get right with God. Yeah, right. There is no God.*

By the following semester of college, I decided to drop out. The president of another area of my company asked me if I'd like to work in the real estate department as a computer programmer, and I agreed to the change. I now woke up drinking and went to bed with booze as well. My life had become an endless cycle of work, alcohol and drugs. I managed to stay afloat, convincing myself I was a functional alcoholic. But inside, I knew better.

In June 2002, a woman named Jessie flew in to train us on some new software. The moment I laid eyes on her, I was completely taken aback by her beauty. She wore a floral sundress, and she was also eight months pregnant. I learned she was married. But even after she flew back to her home in North Carolina, I could not get her striking face out of my mind.

In August, I went out drinking, hitting up my favorite bar where everyone knew my name. The place had become my own personal *Cheers*, and the bartenders never cut me off. After pounding a ton of beers and shots,

THE KID IN BLACK

I stumbled outside. The bouncer, Tiny, who was anything but what his name implied, stared at me inquisitively.

"You all right to drive, bro?" he asked.

I nodded, my eyes glassy as I mustered a smile. "Yeah, I'm fine, man."

I climbed into my car and started the engine. As I made the five-mile drive home, the car crawled along at under 35 miles per hour. I had driven drunk many times before, but I'd always found my way home, even if I didn't remember the trip the next day. Something felt different this time, however. I struggled to focus my eyes on the road, and a trip that should have taken just minutes took nearly an hour. When I returned to my parents' house where I'd been staying, I had trouble parking in the driveway. I awkwardly cranked the wheel, turned the car around and parked it next to the pool.

As I yanked the keys out of the ignition, I stared up at the sky. A full moon hovered brightly in the sky, a radiant ball of beauty above me. Though it was August, a typically muggy month, the night had grown eerily cold. Suddenly, it was as if I was looking down at myself from up above. I climbed out of the car and stumbled toward the house, glancing up at the moon again.

"God, if you are real, prove it!" I cried into the sky.

And just like that, something ignited inside me. It was not a blaze, but instead, a tiny spark, like a Boy Scout's attempt at a campfire after rubbing two little sticks together. I didn't know what it all meant, but I knew it meant something.

The following month, Jessie and I began talking over MSN Instant Messenger. She told me that she'd had her baby but that she'd also learned her husband was cheating on her. Their marriage was over.

I told her I was sorry, and we developed a friendship online. The more we talked, the more I got to like her. *She's beautiful on the inside as well as the outside. I really like this girl.*

In October, Jessie came down to Florida to do more training for my company, and we went out on our first date. Things felt just as natural as they did online, and I enjoyed every minute of our time together. She flew back to North Carolina, and we continued to talk. In November, my boss asked me if I wanted to move to North Carolina to work with another programmer.

"Are you kidding? Of course!" I didn't have to think twice. I'd get a chance to be near Jessie and spend time with her every day. Things couldn't get much better than that!

I relocated to North Carolina. Jessie wanted to take things slowly, however.

"I think we should start off by seeing each other just once a week," she suggested. "But on Sundays, I go to church. If you want to join me, you're welcome to."

I jumped at the opportunity to spend more time with her. *I don't care where this girl goes, I'll follow her.* I knew Jessie was a Christian, and she knew I was not. I told her I wasn't sure how I felt about God. She just smiled and said she was glad I'd be coming to church with her on Sunday.

THE KID IN BLACK

I'll never set foot in a church again! I remembered my indignant words to my well-meaning friends years before. I'd convinced myself I didn't want anything to do with people who called themselves Christians. After witnessing one senseless tragedy after the next, I'd decided God couldn't possibly exist. But something had shifted in me that night beneath that full moon, and a spark was lit where there'd been only darkness for years. *Is it possible that God is real?*

I began attending church with Jessie, and though it was quite large, it wasn't nearly as scary as I imagined. Everyone was extremely friendly, and I enjoyed the pastor's encouraging messages, too. But I still wasn't quite sure this God stuff was for me.

On New Year's Eve, Jessie and I made plans to go out. But she called at the last minute to cancel. "I'm really sorry, Trevor, but I feel like I'm cheating on my ex by dating you. I just feel like I need to spend the night in prayer instead."

I was disappointed but understood. "No problem," I said.

Jessie called the next morning to tell me she'd worked through some stuff. "I realized I had to let my old life go," she explained. "I feel a peace about everything now, and I want to be with you."

Her words greatly excited me. I'd wanted to be with her since the moment I'd laid eyes on her, but I would patiently wait things out. Jessie was a girl worth waiting for.

FREEDOM STORIES

One Sunday, I attended church with Jessie. As I sat in the pew, the loud rock music echoing from the stage, something strange and beautiful happened to me. It was as if everything in the room dulled around me, until I felt as if I was the only person there. The music became nothing but background noise, and the sea of faces surrounding me suddenly blurred. In that moment, I am convinced I met Jesus.

People can meet Jesus in different ways. Some experience a radical life-changing moment. Some feel something quiet in their spirit, a nudging of sorts. For me, it was simple. Jesus came into my heart, into all the broken places of my life, and in that instant, I believed he was real. All my questions were suddenly answered, and I trusted without a doubt there was a God. Light replaced darkness, peace replaced angst, contentment replaced emptiness. The feeling was nearly inexplicable. But I accepted it as absolutely, 100 percent real.

When I walked out of the church service that morning, I no longer had any urge to do drugs, drink or smoke. The desires had been completely removed. I was free of it all, and it felt amazing. *Thank you, God! Oh, thank you!*

I went home, hardly able to wipe the smile off my face. I threw away every ounce of booze and drugs I had. From that moment on, I've been completely clean. I did not have withdrawals or lay awake at night pining for a drink or a hit. The desire was simply gone. I believe this could only be the work of God, as I know no other way to explain such a thing. I'd been an addict for years, fearing I might never get my life back on track. Drugs and booze had nearly ruined my life and almost cost me several jobs. Even when I'd hit rock bottom before moving from Michigan, I still hadn't been able to give up my destructive ways. But now, with the power of Jesus in me, I felt free of everything that had trapped me for so long. What an amazing feeling!

I told Jessie about what Jesus had done in my heart, and she celebrated with me. Over the next few months, we continued to date and grow closer. I began reading my Bible and really understanding the verses I'd once skimmed over. I discovered immense treasure between the pages, viewing the Bible as a love story from God to his children. One story especially stood out to me.

In Matthew 9, Jesus approached a crippled man lying on a mat. He said to him, "My friend, don't worry! Your sins are forgiven." He then told the man to pick up his mat and go home. The man got up and went home, and the crowds around Jesus praised God.

I am the crippled man, I realized, awed by the story. *I was the epitome of ugly and evil. Jesus believed in me, even when I did not believe in him. He has forgiven me for all the hurtful, awful things I've done, and he has been there all along.*

Something else about the story of the crippled man struck me, however. Jesus told him to get up and take his mat. He did not tell him to leave his mat behind. *I think he wanted him to carry his mat so people would know his story of healing and forgiveness. I need to take my mat with me and share my story with the world. God is still writing it, and there is someone who needs to hear it.*

In October of 2003, I asked Jessie to marry me. We married the following May in a beautiful old castle-like building in North Carolina. Her sons, Jimmy, age 5, Harry, age 3, and her daughter, Lily, almost 2, stood beside us as we recited our vows. Next to meeting Jesus, it was the happiest day of my life.

A year later, we felt God was leading Jessie to return to teaching school, her first love. In August, she landed a teaching job. That fall, I sensed things weren't going well at my company. Though my bosses assured me nothing was wrong, I still felt uneasy.

In November, I left and began a new job in South Carolina. A month later, I learned that if I had stayed at my previous company, I would have been laid off. The company was shutting its doors. I thanked God for his provision and for giving me the ability to discern what to do.

I stayed at my new company for the next four years, commuting back and forth from our home in North Carolina. In 2011, I sensed that I needed to move on again. I began applying for jobs in my field all over the East Coast, but nothing turned up. I continued praying and felt God was asking me to expand my territory. At last, I conceded. *Okay, God. I'm open to going wherever you want me to go, even if it means some unknown place on the West Coast. I'm going to let go of control and trust in you. What do you want?*

THE KID IN BLACK

Not long after I expanded my search, I received a phone call from a company in Austin, Texas.

I interviewed, and the hiring manager called back right away and offered me a job.

This is crazy, God! Austin, Texas, was never on my radar, but I trust this is where you want me to go!

"Austin, Texas," I told Jessie. "Looks like another adventure!"

Jessie began applying for teaching jobs in the Austin area but learned they were hard to come by. And then, in an amazing turn of events, she landed a job just outside of Round Rock, where we'd decided to settle. It was nothing short of a miracle, and we thanked God for his impeccable timing.

I know this is definitely what you want for us, God. You've made that abundantly clear!

I moved to Texas in April 2011, and Jessie and the kids followed in June. A few weeks after settling in, we discovered Freedom Church in Round Rock.

Much smaller than the large churches we attended on the East Coast, the church offered a sense of intimacy I appreciated. Everyone welcomed us with open arms, and we discovered authenticity inside those doors.

This is a place for real people from all sorts of backgrounds, a place for people just like me!

I began meeting with Pastor Benito and enjoyed his wisdom and caring heart. "I prayed and felt God tell me I'm supposed to pour into you, Trevor," he told me. "God is going to use you in a mighty way."

Pastor Benito's words excited me. I thought again about the crippled man on the mat. *I know my story isn't over, God. You healed a broken man like me, and if you want to use me, I'm all yours.*

In August 2013, I began online classes at a Bible college with the intent to pursue ministry. Pastor Benito continued to encourage me. "You need a Paul in front of you and a Timothy behind you," he reminded me, referring to two men in the Bible. Paul had mentored and encouraged many young men, and Timothy had looked up to people like Paul. I was a Timothy right now, absorbing as much as I could, learning how to live my life fully dedicated to God. But I hoped in time I could become a Paul, pouring back into young men just like me, reminding them that their stories are not over yet.

Even though I didn't always believe in God, he has always been with me. I believe it was him nudging me to put my seatbelt on during that fast car ride, whispering in my ear during the times I wanted to take my own life and protecting me from the terrible consequences I could have endured due to my drinking and drug abuse.

I often think back to that angry, misunderstood kid with the long hair and the black t-shirts, the kid who announced to the world that he didn't believe in God. I'd been convinced that a loving God would never allow evil and hardship into the world. I'd been convinced Christians were nothing but a bunch of hypocrites. But having been at Freedom Church for more than two years now, I understand that's not the case at all. Christians are real people just like me, folks who have been broken, hurt and beat up by the world, folks who have endured pain and injured others as well.

Life may continue to beat us up, but because of Jesus, we will simply pick up our mats and march on. And we will keep telling the story.

CONCLUSION

When we founded Freedom Church, our desire was to start a church where people, no matter what they were facing, would EXPERIENCE the life-changing power of Jesus Christ and the freedom that only he can bring.

As I read this book, I saw that vision being fulfilled. However, at Freedom Church, rather than being content with what God has done and with our past victories, we believe that there are many more stories of freedom to come.

It seems every time I go out to dinner with people of Freedom Church, they tell me their own stories of how Jesus has dramatically changed their lives. I am reminded that God really loves people, and he is actively seeking to change lives. Think about it: How did you get this book? We believe you read this book because God brought it to you. He is seeking to reveal his love to you. Whether you're a man or a woman, a teacher or a student, a parent or an empty nester, a business owner or employee at Dell, we believe God came to FREE you. He came to FREE us. He FREES us from the hellish pain we've wallowed in. He offers real joy and the opportunity to share in life that will last forever through faith in Jesus Christ.

Do you believe that such radical change is possible? It seems too good to be true, doesn't it? Each of us at FREEDOM CHURCH warmly invites you to come and check out our church family. Freely ask questions, examine our statements and see if we're "for real." If you choose, journey with us at whatever pace you are comfortable. You will find that we are far from perfect. We are all "jacked-up" people who have encountered a perfect God. Our scars and sometimes open wounds are still healing, and we want you to know that God is still completing the process of authentic life change in us. We still make mistakes in our journey, like everyone will. Therefore, we acknowledge our continued need for each other's forgiveness and support. We need the love of God just as much as we did the day before we believed in him.

If you are unable to be with us, yet you intuitively sense you would really like to experience such a life change, here are some basic thoughts to consider. If you choose, at the end of this conclusion, you can pray the suggested prayer. If your prayer genuinely comes from your heart, you will experience the beginning stages of authentic life change, similar to those you have read about.

How does this change occur?

Recognize that what you're doing isn't working. Accept the fact that Jesus desires to forgive you for your bad decisions and selfish motives. Realize that without this forgiveness, you will continue a life separated from God and his amazing love. In the Bible, the book of Romans, chapter 6, verse 23 reads that the result of sin (seeking our way rather than God's way) is death, but the gift that God freely gives is "everlasting life found in Jesus Christ."

CONCLUSION

Believe in your heart that God passionately loves you and wants to give you a new heart. Ezekiel 11:19 reads, "I will give them singleness of heart and put a new spirit within them. I will take away their stony, stubborn heart and give them a tender, responsive heart" (NLT).

Believe in your heart that "if you confess with your mouth that Jesus is Lord and believe in your heart that God raised him from the dead, you will be saved" (Romans 10:9 NLT).

Believe in your heart that because Jesus paid for your failure and wrong motives, and because you asked him to forgive you, he has filled your new heart with his life in such a way that he transforms you from the inside out. Second Corinthians 5:17 reads, "When someone becomes a Christian, he becomes a brand new person inside. He is not the same anymore. A new life has begun!"

Why not pray now?

Lord Jesus, if I've learned one thing in my journey, it's that you are God and I am not. My choices have not resulted in the happiness I hoped they would bring. Not only have I experienced pain, I've also caused it. I know I am separated from you, but I want that to change. I am sorry for the choices I've made that have hurt myself and others and denied you. I believe your death paid for my sins, and you are now alive to change me from the inside out. Would you please do that now? I ask you to come and live in me so that I can sense you are here with me. Thank you for hearing and changing me. Now please help me know when you are talking to me, so I can cooperate with your efforts to change me. Amen.

Round Rock's unfolding story of God's love is still being written … and your name is in it.

I hope to see you this Sunday!

Pastor Benito and Jennifer Fresquez
Freedom Church
Round Rock, Texas

We would love for you to join us at Freedom Church!

We meet Sunday mornings at 9:30 and 11 a.m. at
1205 Round Rock Avenue, Suite 109
Round Rock, TX 78681.

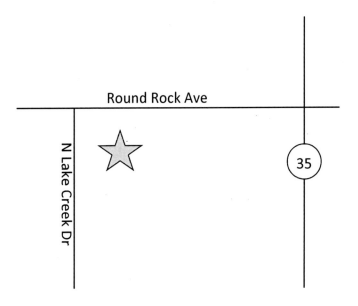

Please call us at 512.431.9859 for directions,
or contact us at www.freetobechurch.com.

For more information on reaching your city with
stories from your church, go to
www.testimonybooks.com.

GOOD CATCH
PUBLISHING

Did one of these stories touch you?
Did one of these real people move you to tears?
Tell us (and them) about it on our Facebook page at
www.facebook.com/GoodCatchPublishing.